POLLENTIA

A Roman Colony on the Island of Mallorca

Norman A. Doenges

BAR International Series 1404

2005

Published in 2016 by
BAR Publishing, Oxford

BAR International Series 1404

Pollentia: A Roman Colony on the Island of Mallorca

ISBN 978 1 84171 845 3

BAR Publishing is the trading name of British Archaeological Reports (Oxford) Ltd.
British Archaeological Reports was first incorporated in 1974 to publish the BAR
Series, International and British. In 1992 Hadrian Books Ltd became part of the BAR
group. This volume was originally published by Archaeopress in conjunction with
British Archaeological Reports (Oxford) Ltd / Hadrian Books Ltd, the Series principal
publisher, in 2005. This present volume is published by BAR Publishing, 2016.

Printed in England

BAR
PUBLISHING

BAR titles are available from:

BAR Publishing
122 Banbury Rd, Oxford, OX2 7BP, UK
EMAIL   info@barpublishing.com
PHONE   +44 (0)1865 310431
FAX   +44 (0)1865 316916
www.barpublishing.com

TABLE OF CONTENTS

	Page
Table of Contents	i
List of Illustrations	iii
Preface	v

Chapter 1
HISTORY, DISCOVERY, AND EARLY EXCAVATIONS

1.1 History	1
1.2 Discovery and Identification of Pollentia	3
1.3 Intervention of the William L. Bryant Foundation	5
1.4 The Roman Theater	6
1.5 The Sa Portella Excavations	6
1.5.1 House of the Bronze Head	8
1.5.2 House of the Two Treasures	8
1.5.3 North House	9
1.5.4 North-South Steet	9
1.5.5 Northwest House	10
1.5.6 City Wall	10
1.6 The Size of Pollentia	11
1.7 Government Protection	12

Chapter 2
THE FORUM OF POLLENTIA

2.1 Overview	13
2.2 The Capitolium	14
2.3 Northeast Temple or Monument	16
2.4 East Temple	17
2.5 Open Area of the Forum	18
2.6 West Side of the Forum	18
2.7 Inscriptions	20
2.8 Final Phases	21
2.9 Forum Necropolis	21
2.10 North of the Capitolium	22

Chapter 3
DARTMOUTH COLLEGE SECTOR

3.1 Dartmouth College Excavations	23
3.2 Overview	23
3.3 The Western Unit: Rooms V, X, and Y	24
3.3.1 The West Street	24
3.3.2 Room Y	26

3.3.3 Room X   29

3.3.4 Room V   34

3.4 The East Unit   38

3.4.1 Room U   39

3.4.2 Room U1   39

3.4.3 Room U2   41

3.4.4 Room Q   42

3.4.5 Room T   43

3.4.6 Room R   45

3.5 Summary   47

Chapter 4
POLLENTIA EXCAVATIONS 1995-2000

4.1 Changes in Leadership   50
4.2 Overview   50
4.3 Room Z   50
4.4 West Street and Portico   52
4.5 Room A   55
4.6 Room B   56
4.7 Sounding West of the Capitolium   57
4.8 Late Fortification System   57
4.9 Forum Pavements and Late South Room   58

Chapter 5
POLLENTIA: HISTORY AND COINAGE

History and Coinage   60
Conspectus of Excavation Coins, 1974-1990   62

BIBLIOGRAPHY   71

LIST OF ILLUSTRATIONS

Fig. 1.1: Location of Pollentia on the peninsula between the Bay of Pollensa and the Bay of Alcudia. 2
Fig. 1.2: The area occupied by the city of Pollentia with the names of the properties over the site. 4
Fig. 1.3: William J. Bryant, President of the William L Bryant Foundation, Woodstock, Vermont. 5
Fig. 1.4: The Roman Theater. 7
Fig. 1.5: Sa Portella 7
Fig. 1.6: Bronze head of a young girl found in the House of the Bronze Head. 8
Fig. 1.7: The House of Polymnia in Camp d'en França. 11

Fig. 2.1: Pollentia Forum. 13
Fig. 2.2: The Capitolium. 14
Fig. 2.3: The Northeast temple or Monument. 17
Fig. 2.4: The East Temple or Temple II. 18
Fig. 2.5: Shops along the west side of the Forum. 19
Fig. 2.6: The Forum Necropolis. 21
Fig. 2.7: Bronze bull figurine found in Room 01 north of the Capitolium. 22

Fig. 3.1: Bryant Foundation-Dartmouth College Sector. 23
Fig. 3.2: View of the Dartmouth Sector from the northeast. In the foreground are Rooms Q, U1, and U2.
    Beyond are Rooms V, X, and Y. 24
Fig. 3.3: Late built corner and *opus signinum* pavement over the West Street. 25
Fig. 3.4: Sampling of pottery found in destruction fill throughout the sector. 28
Fig. 3.5: Iron window grate. 29
Fig. 3.6: Snail Shell Pits in Rooms Y and X. 30
Fig. 3.7: Cylindrical bone hinge. 31
Fig. 3.8: One of the amphorae found on the floor of Room X. 32
Fig. 3.9: Handle from a bronze jug. 33
Fig. 3.10: Small frying pan found at the southeast corner of Room X. 34
Fig. 3.11: Bronze statuette of Mercury. 38
Fig. 3.12: Ten blue glass paste disks. 41
Fig. 3.13: Fish swimming right. 41
Fig. 3.14: ACTIACI seal stamp ring. 42
Fig. 3.15: Roof tile and two *dolia* embedded in first century A. D. surface in Room T. 44
Fig. 3.16: Green glass crater from the south *dolium* in Room T. 44
Fig. 3.17: Bronze statuette of seated figure. 45
Fig. 3.18: Bronze coiled snake. 45

Fig. 4.1: Room Z and West Portico. 51
Fig. 4.2: Cistern in the West Portico. 53
Fig. 4.3: View of Portico drain. 54
Fig. 4.4: View of lower walkway drain. 55
Fig. 4.5: Rooms A and B. 55
Fig. 4.6: Covered oval catch basin in Room A. 56
Fig. 4.7: Location of the sounding between Room C and the Altar. 58

Preface

Excavation of the Roman colony of Pollentia under the auspices of the William L. Bryant Foundation of Woodstock, Vermont, began in 1957 with Dr. Antonio Arribas of the University of the Balearic Islands, Dr. Miguel Tarradell of the University of Barcelona, and Prof. Daniel E. Woods of Manhattanville College, Purchase, NY, serving as directors. The initial effort was limited to the property Sa Portella immediately south of the city of Alcudia, Mallorca, where three atrium-style houses were uncovered. They were published by the directors in two *Memoriae*, nos. 75 (1973) and 98 (1978), in the series *Excavaciones Arqueológicas en España* of the Servicio Nacional de Excavaciones in Madrid. After 1963 attention turned to the search for and excavation of the Forum of Pollentia. Annual campaigns during the summer months in the area of the Forum were initiated in 1980 on the property Ca'n Reinés and continue to this day. A brief preliminary report on the excavations appeared in 1987, but a full account has never been published, and sadly much of the record has been lost over time.

The purpose of this monograph is to give a brief history of early investigations on the site, to summarize the Sa Portella excavations, the reports on which are now out of print, and to present an account in English of the discoveries in the Forum area of the city. Aspects of the work there have appeared in articles in either Spanish or Catalan, but there has been no overall treatment of the site. Special attention is given to the efforts of a team from Dartmouth College under the direction of Norman A. Doenges which excavated a series of rooms in the *insula* west of the forum from 1986 to 1995. Although a final report on the excavations was submitted to the directors, there has been no reference to the work of the Dartmouth team in any publication relating to Pollentia. Hence a description of the Dartmouth sector of the excavations appears here for the first time. So also does the study of the coins found in the Forum area by Prof. Harold B. Mattingly of the University of Leeds.

The author wishes to express his gratitude to Antonio Arribas, who served as lead director of the excavation after 1980 and who approved the participation of the Dartmouth College team in the effort at Pollentia. But special recognition must be given to William J. Bryant, president of the William L. Bryant Foundation, for his generous support of the Pollentia excavations in all their aspects and his promotion of the Bryant Foundation-Dartmouth College Archaeological Internship Program on the site. Fifty-three Dartmouth College undergraduate students participated in the program from 1982 to 1995, almost all of whom had their first taste of field archaeology at Pollentia. Several have gone on to become professional archaeologists, classicists, or art historians.

Excavation at Pollentia continues under the direction of Dra. Margarita Orfila Pons of the University of Granada. Work centers in the open area of the Forum with special attention to problems of dating and study of the modular plan of the city. Chapter 4 dealing with campaigns from 1995 to 2000 is the result of close communication and fruitful collaboration with Dra. Orfila.

Norman A. Doenges
Hanover, NH

POLLENTIA

Chapter 1

HISTORY, DISCOVERY, AND EARLY EXCAVATIONS

1.1 History

The Roman city of Pollentia is located on the north coast of the Mediterranean island of Mallorca 53 klm. north-northeast from Palma. It occupies a slight rise now covered with a series of almond groves immediately south of the modern city of Alcudia, Mallorca. Like the modern city it was strategically placed on an isthmus between two expansive bays, the Bahía de Alcudia and the Bahía de Pollença. Both bays are protected by mountainous Cape Formentor from prevailing northwest winds and provide excellent shelter to shipping. (Fig. 1.1)

Pollentia was founded along with Palma, according to Strabo 3.5.1, by Q. Caecilius Metellus Balearicus following a campaign against Mediterranean pirates operating from the Balearic Islands of Mallorca and Menorca. Livy, *Ep.* 60, indicates that Metellus undertook the campaign as consul in 123 B.C. In recognition of his victory over the pirates and for adding the Baleares to the Empire he celebrated a triumph in Rome in 121 B.C. The two cities would thus have been established, according to the written sources, after the pacification of Mallorca probably in 122 B.C.

It is not clear why the senate saw fit to commission one of the consuls for the year 123 B.C. to conduct a minor campaign overseas when Rome itself was in turmoil over the political machinations of the tribune C. Sempronius Gracchus. But Metellus' expedition was perhaps part of a larger program of pacification in the northwest basin of the Mediterranean which began in 126 B.C. In that year the senate dispatched the consul L. Aurelius Orestes with C. Gracchus serving as his quaestor to Sardinia to quell a major rebellion on the island. It took the consul four years to suppress the revolt. In 125 B.C. the consul M. Fulvius Flaccus was detailed to Transalpine Gaul to push the Ligurians and Saluvii Gauls out of the territory of Massilia. He was followed by a succession of consuls, C. Sextius Calvinus in 124 B.C., L. Domitius Ahenobarbus in 122 B.C., and Q. Fabius Maximus in 121 B.C. They successively crushed the Saluvii and Allobroges east of the Rhone and then the Arverni west of the Rhone.[1] The objective of these campaigns was to relieve pressure from the Gauls on the city of Massilia and to establish a secure land route from Italy to Spain. Operations ended with the formation of the province of Gallia Narbonensis in southern France. As part of his campaign Sextius

Calvinus moved the Saluvii back from the Mediterranean coast, settling them inland one and a half miles from the sea. He also established what Strabo 4.1.5 calls a guard post of veterans over the Saluvii at Aquae Sextiae (Aix en Provence). Strabo 3.5.1 says that although the inhabitants of the Balearic Islands were as a people peaceful a few evil-doers among them joined with the Mediterranean pirates to bring the islanders into disrepute. The fact that the islands became a base for the pirates brought the Romans down on them. M. G. Morgan has suggested that the pirates may have been in part Ligurian, Sardinian, and Gallic refugees from Rome's campaigns in Sardinia and Gaul who fled to the Baleares. With support from the islanders they raided shipping between Italy, Gaul, and Spain and kept opposition to the Romans in Gaul and Sardinia alive.[2] It is possible that Metellus went to Spain to deal with the situation there, serving not only as consul but also as proconsul of Hispania Citerior.[3] Operating from Spain, he defeated the pirates off the islands in a major sea battle in which he protected his ships from the shots of the Balearic slingers by stretching hides over their decks. Thus some islanders fought with the pirates against the Romans.

Strabo says that, after pacifying the islands, Metellus founded Palma and Pollentia by bringing as settlers 3,000 "*Romaioi*" from Spain. It is difficult to know precisely what Strabo meant by the designation "*Romaioi*." But it

---

[1] For the campaigns in Gaul see Livy, *Ep.* 59-61, and Strabo, 4.1.5.

[2] Morgan 1969: 225-226 argues that in authorizing the campaign to the Baleares the senate was not so much influenced by piratical interference with trade to Spain or by pressure from the *equites* in Rome concerned about their commercial interests as by fear that C. Gracchus would attempt to exploit the situation in Spain for his political purposes. The Gracchi had a large *clientela* in Hispania Citerior. As the pirates were raiding the coast of Spain, the senate was fearful that Gaius would raise the issue of trouble in Spain to increase his support among the *equites*. Hence the decision to act in 123 B.C.

[3] So Morgan 1969: 226 who proposes that the war against the pirates and mopping up operations on the islands after the battle would not have kept Metellus in Spain for two years. Duties as proconsul of Hispania Citerior, on the other hand, may have kept him there. Morgan believes that because Rome was already fully engaged in Gaul and Sardinia Metellus did not take troops with him from Italy but recruited his crews and military in Spain. J. S. Richardson 1986: 157 questions whether Metellus served as proconsul of Hispania Citerior although he recognizes that Metellus must have conducted his campaign from the peninsula. L. A. Curchin 1991: 40-41 agrees but points out that if Metellus had not been proconsul taking 3,000 men from Spain to settle on the islands would have been an act of "reprehensible interference" in another's jurisdiction.

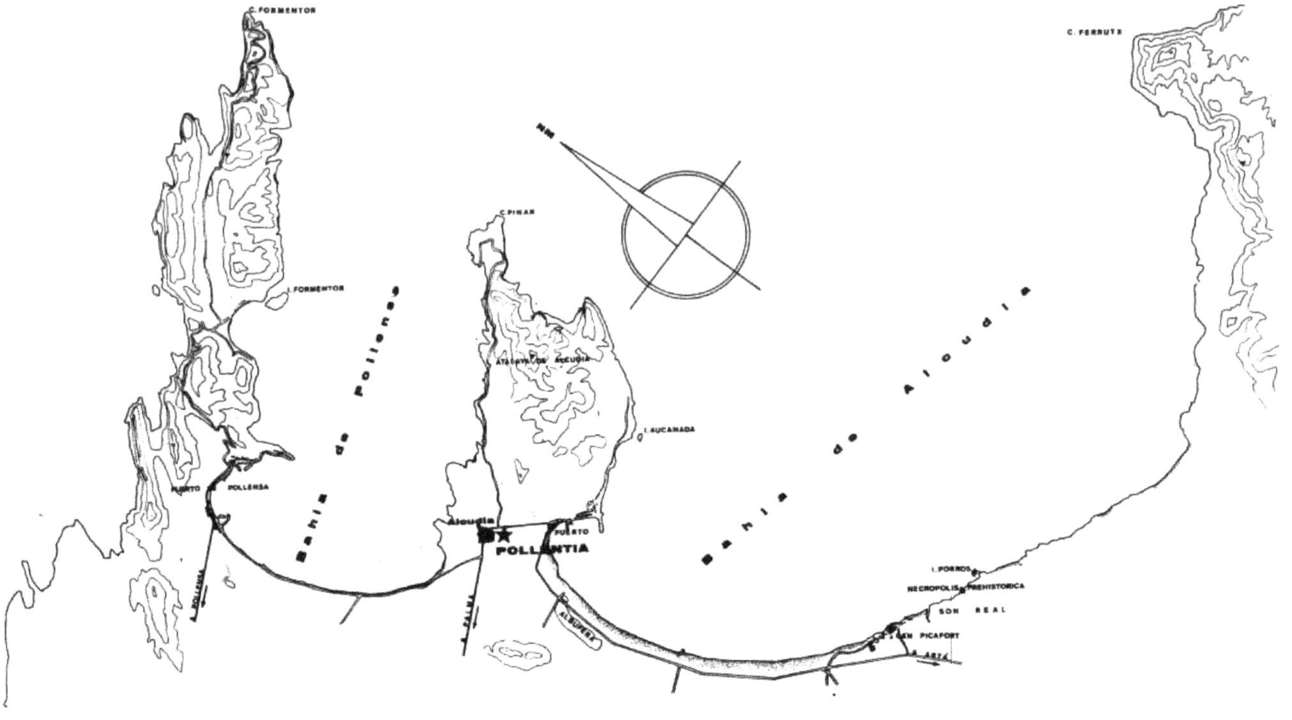

Fig. 1.1 Location of Pollentia on the peninsula between the Bay of Pollença and the Bay of Alcudia.

is unlikely that there were many Roman citizens who had settled in Spain by 123 B.C. and who would have been willing to leave estates on the peninsula for an uncertain life on the Balearic Islands. By "*Romaioi*" Greeks of the late first century B.C. generally meant either Italians, whether or not they were Romans, or Latinized natives of lands outside Italy. It has been opined that the men transferred by Metellus from Spain to the islands were Spanish of mixed native and Italian blood and perhaps veterans of Metellus' campaign.[4]

It is uncertain what the original legal status of Palma and Pollentia was. Pomponius Mela (early 1st century A.D.) 2.24 calls them *coloniae* while Pliny, *NH* 3.5.77, identifies them as *oppida civium Romanorum*. In a careful analysis of Pliny's numbers for the various types of communities in the province of Hispania Tarraconensis Robert Knapp concludes that Palma and Pollentia properly belong on Pliny's list of *coloniae civium Romanorum* from which they were inadvertently omitted.[5] It may well be the case that in Pliny's day in

the first century A.D Palma and Pollentia had the status of *coloniae civium Romanorum*. But if so, they may have been elevated to that status only under Caesar or Augustus in the late first century B.C. The archaeological evidence indicates that there was no planned Roman settlement on the site of Pollentia until the second quarter of the first century B.C. at the earliest although there may have been some Roman presence before that date.[6] There is, indeed, no record in the

individual communities (*NH* 3.3.18-23) only ten Roman colonies are identified. To account for Pliny's total of 179 towns (*NH* 3.3.18) in the province the two settlements on Mallorca have to be added to the list of ten colonies at *NH* 3.3.28, not to the list of *municipia* which are properly tallied. Mallorca and Menorca under the Empire were attached to the province of Hispania Tarraconensis. Knapp rejects the suggestion by A. J. N. Wilson 1966: 22, that the settlements were *municipia civium Romanorum* on the grounds that municipal status was granted to existing native communities, not to new settlements. It does seem to be the case, as Wilson points out, that all of the twelve towns labeled by Pliny as *oppida civium Romanorum* were in fact *municipia* under Augustus. But to include Palma and Pollentia in that list would upset Pliny's count by two *municipia*. Note Knapp's instructive chart on p. 135.

[6] The earliest Roman coins found in the Forum area of Pollentia cluster around 150 B.C. in date. There is then a gap in the sequence until the reign of Augustus. H. B. Mattingly, 1983: 246, and "Pollentia: History and Coinage" (below p. 61) notes that the Roman Republican coinage from Sa Portella and the Forum area resembles that of the Metellan camp of 79 B.C. at Cáceres, not that of the Scipionic camps of 134-33 B.C. at Numantia. The pottery evidence indicates that the earliest

---

[4] For the *Romaioi* settlers in Palma and Pollentia see Strabo 3.5.1. He calls the two settlements cities (*poleis*). R. C. Knapp 1977: 138 argues that the settlers were either *hybridae* of mixed native and Italian blood or natives who had adopted Roman culture. Morgan 1969: 230-231 believes they were predominantly veterans who had served in Metellus' campaign and who remained on the island in a military capacity to keep order.

[5] Knapp 1977: 131-136 points out that Pliny, *NH* 3.3.18, says that there were twelve *coloniae civium Romanorum* in the province of Hispania Tarraconensis but in Pliny's list of

sources that Palma and Pollentia were "founded" formally as colonies. The historical and archaeological evidence suggests that Metellus Balearicus settled the 3,000 *Romaioi* from the mainland at Palma and Pollentia without a formal colonial charter from Rome.[7] They lived, 1500 at each site, either along with native inhabitants or in a military camp attached to the community. Their primary mission was to keep the peace on the island.[8] It is then possible that Q. Caecilius Metellus Pius, grand-nephew of Balearicus, after the Sertorian war (80-71 B.C.) introduced additional settlers, mainly Italian and Spanish veterans who had fought under him in Spain. He may have formally organized the two communities as Latin colonies. It was only at that time that Pollentia became a Roman city with an open forum, permanent structures in stone and mud brick, and streets on a grid pattern.[9] Finally under Augustus when

there was a spurt of building activity on the site additional colonists may have arrived and the status of the settlement was raised to that of a *colonia civium Romanorum* or Roman colony.[10]

1.2 Discovery and Identification of Pollentia

In the late sixteenth century the local antiquarian J. B. Binimelis proposed that the ancient city of Pollentia lay beneath the fields surrounding the chapel of Santa Ana south of Alcudia.[11] But throughout the seventeenth and eighteenth century scholars continued to debate exactly where Pollentia was located whether at Alcudia or beneath the estate of Bócor near Puerto de Pollença twelve kilometers west of Alcudia. At Bócor as in the fields south of Alcudia significant finds of Roman coins and pottery were being made. The name of modern Pollença suggested that the ancient city was situated nearby. It was not until the substantial excavations of Gabriel Llabrés and Rafael Isasi Ransome from 1923 to 1935 that the issue was put to rest and it was established that Pollentia lay at Alcudia.

But even before Llabrés and Isasi began to excavate, the evidence weighed heavily in favor of Alcudia. In either 1687 or 1757 a marble bust of the Emperor Augustus was found in Camp d'en França south of Alcudia.[12] In the early eighteenth century two dedicatory inscriptions, one to Q. Caecilius Catullus and the other to L. Dentilius Modestus, were found in the same field.[13] Additional inscriptions to L. Vibius Nigellio, to Q. Flavius Ponticus, and to Flavia Paulina turned up in the nineteenth century.[14] None of these inscriptions contains the name of the site. Finally in 1887 a small fragment of an inscription was found, the last line of which may refer to the city. The line reads "SP POLL" which has been tentatively restored as [...re]SP(publica) POLL(entina).[15] Throughout the eighteenth and nineteenth centuries coins and other small objects continued to be found in the fields south of Alcudia. But at the beginning of the twentieth century the nature and extent of the Roman

---

Roman structures on the site date no earlier than the first half of the first century B.C.

[7] So Wilson 1966: 22. Knapp 1977: 138 postulates that Metellus Balearicus established the towns as Latin colonies, comparing them to Valentia on the peninsula which may have been settled at about the same time and which he believes without evidence was a Latin colony. A more apt analogue may be Aquae Sextiae, settled by C. Sextius Calvinus, in the same year as the Mallorcan towns. Livy, *Ep.* 61, calls it a *colonia* and Pliny, *NH* 3.4.36, lists it as a Latin colony in his day. But Strabo 4.1.5 states that Calvinus established Aquae Sextiae as a native town (*polis*) to which a garrison (*phroura*) of "*Romaioi*" (Italian) veterans was attached. Metellus may have done the same on Mallorca. Only later ca. 70 B.C. did the communities on Mallorca achieve the status of Latin colonies. Similarly Aquae Sextiae may have achieved Latin status with the settlement of additional veterans in 100 B.C following the victory of Marius at Aquae Sextiae in 102 B.C.

[8] The foundation of a Talayotic (pre-Roman) round house was found beneath the Calle Porticada in the Sa Portella excavations. Beneath Room Y in the Dartmouth sector of the Forum site a Talayotic pavement level and a possible wall of the Talayotic period has been identified. Throughout the forum area there is evidence of Talayotic presence on the site before the construction of the Roman city. In the earliest Roman levels Talayotic pottery in some quantity is found along with Campanian and Roman common wares.

[9] It is also possible that Strabo was in error in naming Metellus Balearicus as the founder of the two cities and that Palma and Pollentia were in fact founded by Metellus Pius as Latin colonies. The evidence on the ground at Pollentia would support such a hypothesis. In 81 B.C. Sertorius briefly occupied Ebusus and fought there a losing naval engagement against the Romans (Plutarch, *Sertorius* 7). Throughout the war Sertorius had the support of pirates operating perhaps from the Balearic Islands against the east coast of Spain. At the end of the war in 71 B.C. Pompey hastily returned to Italy with his men under arms in order to run for the consulship of 70 B.C. Inordinately proud of his victory over Sertorius, Metellus stayed on in Spain, demobilized his legions there, and returned to Rome to celebrate a triumph along with Pompey. See Mattingly 1983: 246. There is no evidence in the sources that Metellus Pius settled veterans at Palma or Pollentia, but Pollentia as an organized community dates from the period of the war against Sertorius.

[10] Mattingly 1983: 246 proposes that Julius Caesar chartered Palma and Pollentia as *municipia civium Romanorum,* but he recognizes that Pollentia experienced major building activity under Augustus. It is unlikely that Palma and Pollentia ever had municipal status. See above note 5.

[11] J. B. Binimelis 1927: vol 1, pp. 72-133, and vol. 2, pp.153-207. The book was first published in 1593.

[12] The date of its discovery is uncertain. Camp d'en França is the older name of the field beneath which lies the Forum area of the city.

[13] C. Veny 1965 no. 25 (=*CIL.* 2.3696) and no. 26 (=*CIL* 2. 3697). Both inscriptions were found in Camp d'en França. Both men served as aediles and *duoviri,* chief magistrates in a Roman colony.

[14] Veny 1965 nos. 27, 28, and 29 (=*CIL* 2.3698, 3699, and 3700).

[15] Veny 1965 no. 24 (=*CIL* 2, Suppl. 5990). For a list of finds, many with dates, in the eighteenth and nineteenth centuries see P. Ventayol Suau, 1927: 39-59.

remains beneath the almond groves still remained a mystery. The excavations of Llabrés and Isasi left no doubt that the site was that of a major provincial Roman city.

Gabriel Llabrés, *Delegado Regio de Bellas Artes* on Mallorca and *Catedrático de Historia del Instituto Balear* in Palma, and Rafael Isasi, artillery colonel, were amateur archaeologists and antiquarians, more interested in finding museum pieces than in conducting a scientific excavation. But Isasi, who was in charge in the field, did keep detailed notebooks with excellent field drawings and sketches.[16] Unfortunately he along with Juan Llabrés, son of Gabriel, published only one formal report of their activities dealing with the campaigns of 1930 and 1931.[17] Because the almond groves over the site were privately owned and were still producing, Isasi had permission to excavate only between the rows of trees. At the end of each campaign the owners required him to refill his trenches. The result was that he was unable to pursue a systematic program of excavation. It was also not possible for him to construct a clear picture of the plan of the city. The excavations thus were from year to year haphazard, dependent on the good will of the owners. Isasi, nevertheless, was an indefatigable excavator, operating with a small army of workmen.[18] He dug extensive trenches in every field around the sanctuary of Santa Ana and recovered a massive quantity of archaeological material each summer. He tended to keep only the coins, jewelry, statuary, and whole pots suitable for display. Fragments were thrown back into the trenches or carted off. Usable building stones were given to the owners or sold.

By the standards of the day Isasi's excavations were highly successful. From 1923 to 1927 the excavators concentrated their efforts in Camp d'en França which they estimated was in the center of the Roman city. (Fig. 1.2) In 1923 they found rooms oriented SE to NW along a street and a bronze statuette of Mercury. Near Santa Ana in that same year they excavated a richly decorated atrium house. In one room of the house was a large polychrome mosaic floor, and amid the burnt rubble over

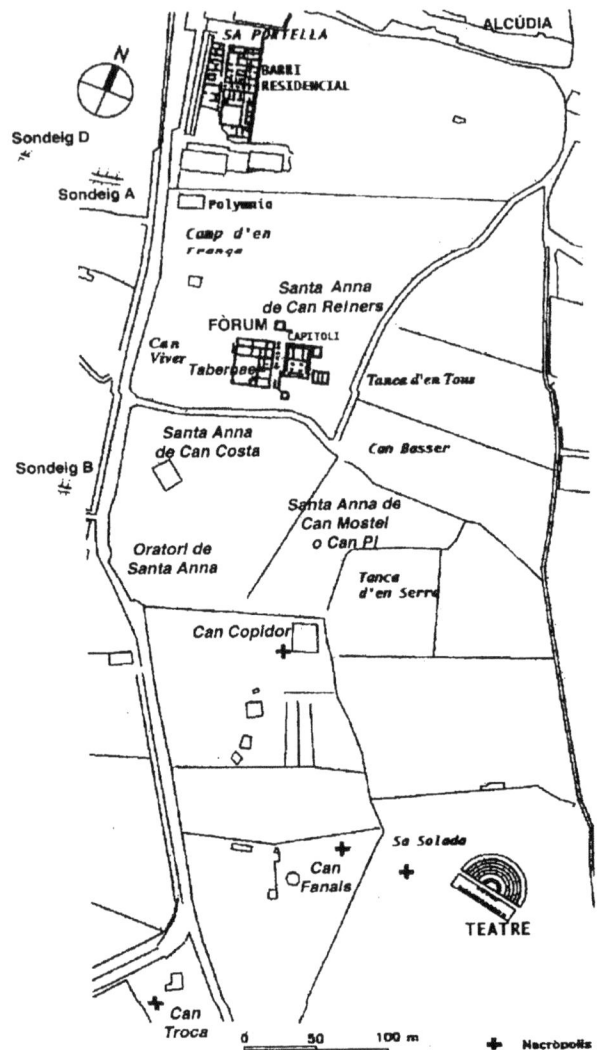

Fig 1.2 The area occupied by the city of Pollentia with the names of the properties over the site.

the floor of the atrium was the life-size head of a bronze horse, 0.52 m. tall, almost certainly from a bronze equestrian statue.[19] The excavators also collected an impressive number of small finds. In 1926 they excavated a well in Camp d'en França from which they recovered a portrait bust of a man in marble, a bronze statuette of Apollo, 0.40 m. tall, a small bronze statuette of a woman, 0.09 m. tall, several fragments of marble statues, and an inscription reading "...Aprilis...Cartago capta fuit."[20] In 1927 Isasi returned to Camp d'en França where he excavated a massive round tower, 6.70 m. in diameter. Nearby he found a marble statuette of a

---

[16] Gabriel Llabrés and Isasi conducted excavations in 1923 and then after a break in 1926 and 1927. Llabrés died in 1928 and was succeded by his son, Juan Llabrés Bernal, who served as an assistant to Isasi in the field. Together they resumed excavation at Pollentia from 1930 to 1935 when the outbreak of the Spanish Civil War interrupted operations. Then from 1944 to 1946 Isasi returned to Pollentia where he conducted minor excavations. Isasi's field notebooks have been preserved by his family. Dra. Mercedes Roca, director of the Pollentia excavations, inspected the notebooks in the summer of 1993.

[17] J. Llabrés Bernal and R. Isasi Ransome 1939. Ventayol Suau 1927: 52-59 gives a brief summary of Isasi's excavations.

[18] Isasi received from the state a subvention of 5,000 pesetas each year, a very substantial sum in the 1920s. The entire amount was devoted to excavation. See A. Arribas and M. Tarradell, 1987: 124, n. 2.

---

[19] For a description see A. García y Bellido 1949: 445, n. 473. The piece is now located in the Museo Arqueológico Nacional in Madrid where it was placed in 1927. The mosaic is in the Bellver Castle in Palma.

[20] For the male head see A. Garcia y Bellido 1951: 53-65. For the inscription see Veny 1965: no. 57. The inscription was sent to Madrid where it disappeared.

woman representing the goddess *Pudicitia*, a bronze statuette of a boy representing Narcissus, and a bronze parade standard.[21] The excavations of 1930 and 1931 centered on the fields adjacent to the chapel of Santa Ana at the south edge of the Roman city. There the excavators dug a late Roman cemetery of 38 graves all in a row. In the graves they found a large number of bronze and gold rings, ear rings, necklaces, and pendants.[22] Beneath the graves was a large building in poor repair and of indeterminate nature. Nearby they uncovered parts of two other large structures, probably houses, and a well-preserved pottery kiln. Finally in the winter of 1934-35, still concentrating on the fields near Santa Ana, Isasi found three life-size marble statues, one of a Roman military commander in a highly decorated cuirass, a second of a Roman matron, and a third of a male figure in a toga.[23] In the area of the cemetery he recovered a funerary inscription partly in verse to Cornelius Atticus, a pancratist, and another to a Christian matron Arguta, who died at age forty.[24] The extent of these excavations and the nature of the finds, especially the inscriptions and the statues, confirmed the fact that there was a major Roman city beneath the almond groves of Alcudia

The onset of the Spanish civil war brought an end to further exploration of the Roman city. But at the beginning of the war in 1936 the fascist *Ramo de Guerra* on Mallorca planned to build a rail line from Sa Pobla south of Alcudia to Alcudia. As part of that project from 1936 to 1938 military engineers dug a huge foundation hole, 75 x 40 m., for the construction of a railroad station at the south end of the property Sa Portella immediately south from the parochial church of Alcudia. The railroad station was never built, but the excavation of the foundation hole to bedrock cut through what seemed to be the west wall of the Roman city and revealed along its north and south sides truncated house walls and at least one mosaic floor. Taking advantage of that situation after the end of the war, two antiquarians and amateur archaeologists, Luis R. Amorós and J. Malberti, in 1944 and again in 1948-1949 conducted exploratory excavations along the north side of the cutting on the property Sa Portella which had been confiscated for the construction of the station and which after the war passed to the control of the Museo Arqueológico in Palma. In 1949 Amorós under authorization from the museum in Barcelona exposed the west face of the Roman city wall along the west side of Sa Portella. The field notes of Amorós have disappeared, but the massive quantity of

pottery from the dig was preserved for study.[25] In 1949-50 Luis Amorós assisted by Samuel Vilaire Turull, a local school teacher, and Jaime Ques, the local priest, excavated another 42 graves in the Ca'n Fanals necropolis near Santa Ana. In 1954 the same team excavated 35 graves behind the old slaughter house northwest from the city. Finally in 1952 another team of amateurs, V. R. Argilés and B. Enseñat Estrany, cleared a large cistern, 13.50 x 4.30 x 5.50 m. deep, immediately adjacent to the chapel of Santa Ana.

Fig. 1.3 William J. Bryant, President of the William L. Bryant Foundation, Woodstock, Vermont.

1.3 Intervention of the William L. Bryant Foundation

Until 1952 exploration of Pollentia was largely in the hands of local enthusiasts. In that year William J. Bryant, president of the William L. Bryant Foundation, brought Pollentia to the attention of professional archaeologists from Barcelona and Madrid.[26] (Fig. 1.3) Early in 1945 Mr. Bryant through the *Sociedad Arqueológica Luliana* in Palma contacted Rafael Isasi with an offer of financial support for his excavations in Alcudia. After an exchange of letters Mr. Bryant in 1946

---

[21] See García y Bellido 1949 for the Narcissus and the bronze standard. Both are now in the Museo Arqueológico Nacional in Madrid.

[22] Much of the jewelry is now on display in the archaeological museum in Barcelona.

[23] For these impressive statues see García y Bellido 1949. They were found together in Ca'n Mustel de Santa Ana and are now displayed in the archaeological museum in Alcudia.

[24] Veny 1965: no. 30 to Cornelius and no. 55 to Arguta.

[25] For the excavations see L. R. Amorós 1944-46 and L. R. Amorós 1947-52. The *terra sigillata* pottery from the 1948-1949 excavations was studied by H. Comfort 1961. The excavators paid no attention to stratigraphy along the wall, but wisely they did collect all of the archaeological materials including pottery sherds. Luis Amorós was a lawyer by profession. Malberti was director of the Museo de Mallorca in Palma.

[26] William J. Bryant died June 13, 1998. For the archaeological and cultural activities of the Bryant Foundation in Spain, Florida, and the Caribbean see Doenges 2005.

sent 20,000 pesetas to Isasi for the excavation of a "trireme" which, Isasi said, had been discovered in the Bahía de Alcudia. Isasi, in fact, used the money at Pollentia but never accounted for the expenditure before his death in 1948. Disappointed, Mr. Bryant turned to a project which he had contemplated undertaking since the early 1930's, the excavation of the Roman amphitheater in Tarragona. Working through the Marqués de Lozoya, *Director General de Bellas Artes* in the Franco government, he underwrote the excavation of the amphitheater from 1948 to 1957. But while work on the Tarragona amphitheater was still in progress, Mr. Bryant in 1951 sent his agent in Spain, José Gonzalez Guijarro, who had been the secretary to the Marqués, to Mallorca to meet with Luis Amorós concerning the Roman theater at Alcudia.[27] The result was that with the help of Guijarro and Amorós Mr. Bryant in 1952 bought the property, Sa Solada, on which the Roman theater of Pollentia was located. In the autumn of that year at the request of Mr. Bryant Dr. Martín Almagro, then Professor of Archaeology at the University of Barcelona, Director of the Archaeological Museum in Barcelona, and Director of the excavations at Ampurias, commissioned Antonio Arribas, Assistant Professor of Archaeology in Barcelona, to excavate the Roman theater. Martín Almagro and Luis Amorós served as directors of the excavation. Samuel Vilaire, the local school master, and Jaime Ques, the parochial priest in Alcudia, assisted Arribas in the field. Buoyed by the success of the excavation, Mr. Bryant decided to direct his attention to the city of Pollentia. To advance his plans, he purchased in 1953 a seventeenth century manor house, centrally located behind the town hall in Alcudia, to serve as the municipal museum of the city and excavation headquarters for future exploration of Pollentia. Finally in 1957 he brought about the formation of a center for archaeological study, the *Centro Arqueológico Hispano-Americano de las Islas Baleares*, located at the house in Alcudia and incorporating the leading archaeologists in Spain, to supervise the excavation of Pollentia. The representatives from Spain included Dr. Almagro, who later moved to the University of Madrid and became Director General of archaeological excavations in Spain, Dr. Luis Pericot, Professor of Prehistory and Dean of the Faculty in Barcelona, and Dr. Miguel Tarradell, Professor of Archaeology in Valencia and later in Barcelona. American representatives included Dr. Walter Cook of the Institute of Fine Arts in New York University, Prof. Sterling Dow of Harvard University, and Prof. Daniel E. Woods of Manhattanville College. Collaboration between Spanish and American archaeologists continued until 1997 within the framework of the Center and from 1982 onward through an agreement between the Department of Classics at Dartmouth College and the directors of the excavations at Pollentia.

1.4 The Roman Theater

The Catalan archaeologist Francisco Martorell y Peña was the first scholar to recognize in 1887 the existence of a theater on the site of Pollentia. In 1923 Isasi removed a modern wall which ran over the *cavea* of the theater, but his interest was diverted from it to what seemed to be the center of the city. Using a plan of the theater drawn by Isasi, the Italian scholar Luigi Bernabò Brea, who visited the site in 1951, declared it to be of Greek type with a circular orchestra, the last such theater known from the ancient world. The excavations of Antonio Arribas and Luis Amorós undertaken in 1952 with the support of the Bryant Foundation, however, confirmed that the theater is Roman in plan with a semi-circular orchestra. (Fig. 1.4)

The theater is located at the southeast corner of the city. The orchestra is 9.50 m. in diameter, and there is evidence that it was originally paved with concrete. Behind the orchestra are three rows of backed seats comprising the *proedria*. The first or lowest row of seats is separated from the two above by a narrow *praecinctio* or ambulatory. Between the *proedria* section and the *cavea* is a broader *praecinctio*, 1.20 m. wide. Still preserved on its east side but in very poor repair are eleven rows of seats of the *cavea* which is divided into four *cunei*. Cuttings in bedrock identify the location of the *proscenium* and the *scaena*. In the *proscenium* are five square holes probably for insertion of posts to support a raised wooden stage. The overall diameter of the theater was at least 75 m. It may have held as many as two thousand persons.[28]

Arribas dates the theater to the early first century A.D. After it fell into disuse, late Roman and early-Christian graves were dug in the *scaena* and in the east side of the *cavea*.

1.5 The Sa Portella Excavations

Through the efforts of Luis Pericot, who as Professor of Prehistory in Barcelona was responsible for archaeological exploration on Mallorca, the Bryant Foundation was granted permission to conduct excavations on the property Sa Portella which had been appropriated by the state for the construction of the Sa Pobla-Alcudia railroad station and which was in the 1950s under the control of the Museo de Mallorca in Palma. Excavation on the site began in 1957 under the direction of Miguel Tarradell and Daniel Woods, both representing the Center. They were joined in 1958 by Antonio Arribas from Barcelona. The objective was for the first time to make use of the latest archaeological

---

[27] After the death of Isasi Luis Amorós was named *Comisario de Excavaciones* for the island of Mallorca.

[28] For the theater see L. R. Amorós, M. Almagro, and A. Arribas 1954a and L. R. Amorós, M. Almagro, and A. Arribas 1954b.

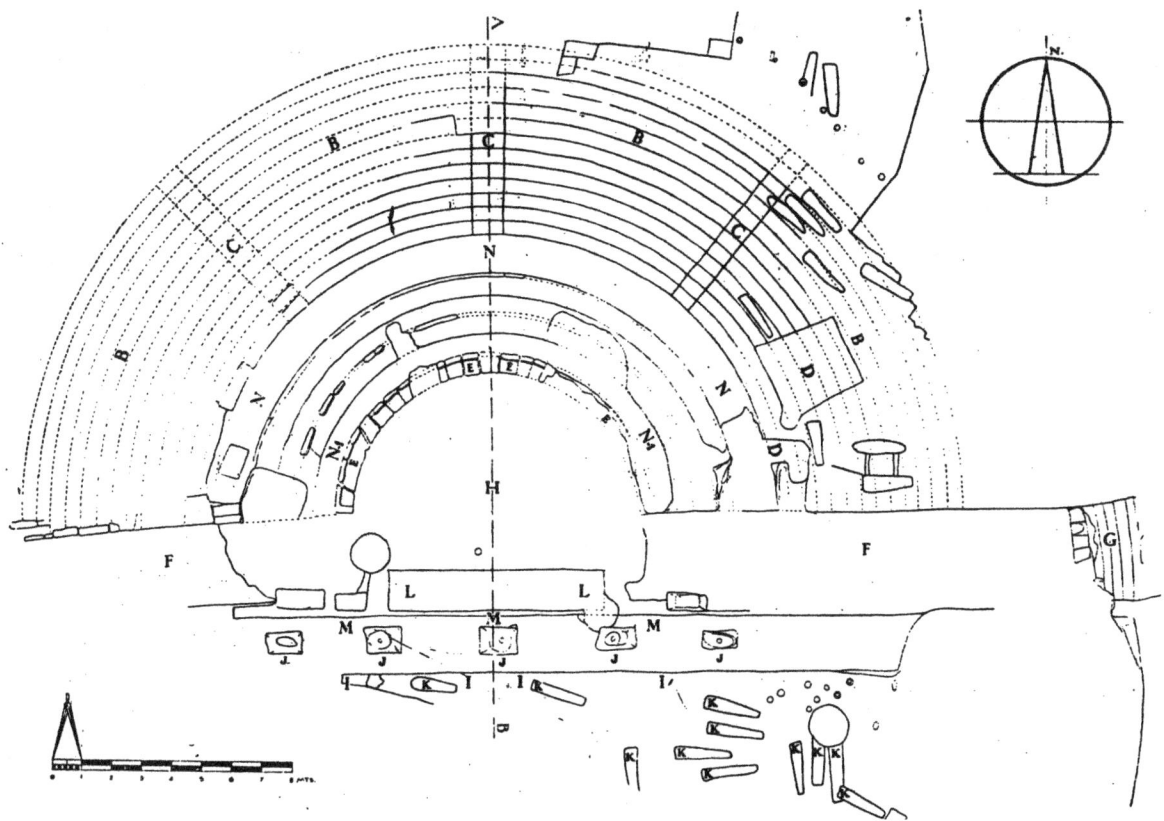

Fig. 1.4 The Roman Theater

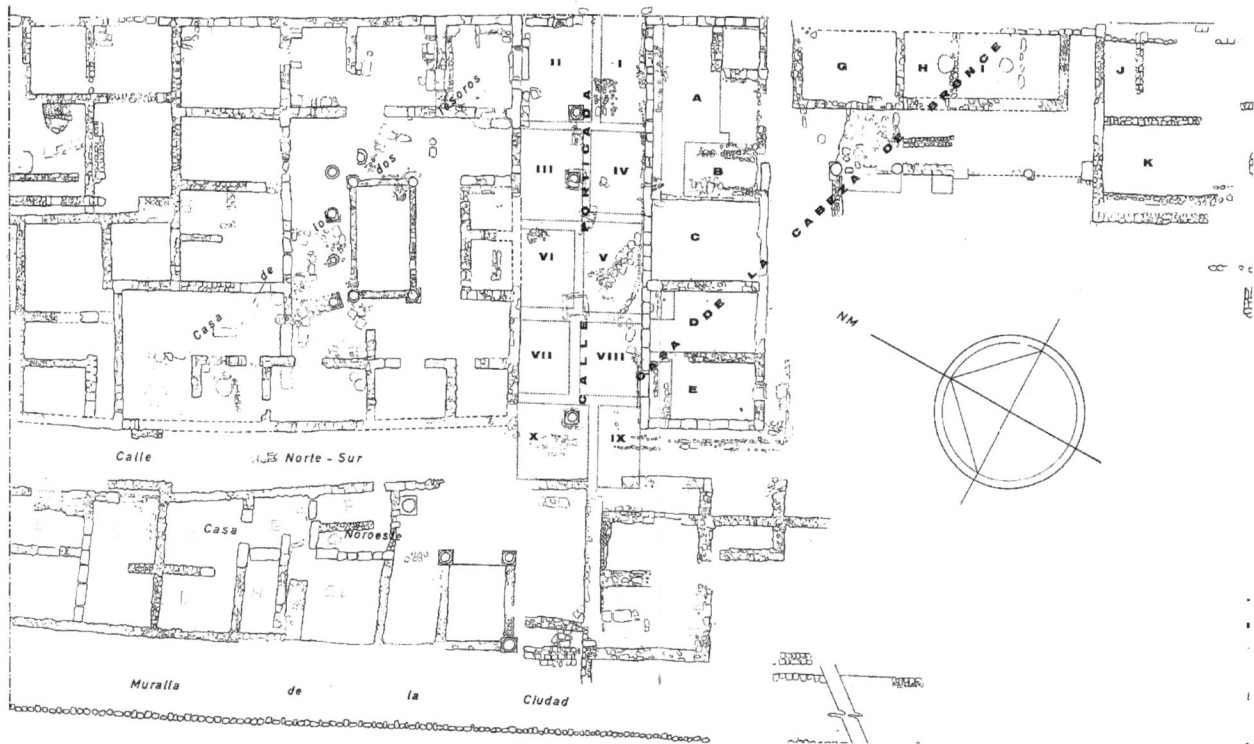

Fig. 1.5 Sa Portella

methods to extract as much information as possible from the only area of the city then available for investigation. The excavations were conducted annually during the summer months from 1957 to 1962. They uncovered a residential area of the ancient city, specifically three atrium style houses at the intersection of two streets and part of a fourth house.[29] (Fig. 1.5)

Fig. 1.6 Bronze head of a young girl found in the House of the Bronze Head

1.5.1 House of the Bronze Head

The southernmost of the three houses, the House of the Bronze Head, was found to be in very poor repair. Only the north wall of the house, five rooms along its north side, and five rooms along the east side facing a peristyle courtyard are intact and could be usefully studied. The entire south side of the structure was destroyed during the excavation of the railroad station cutting. The house measures 22.50 m. west to east and may have extended 32 m. north to south. The northeast corner of the peristyle survives along with the pedestals and bases of three columns along its east side. A low wall ran between the columns. The cushioned ashlar north wall of the house

along the Colonnaded Street is its most striking feature. In the northeast corner of Room D on the north side of the house amid a pile of burnt rubble the bronze head of a young girl (Fig. 1.6) was found together with two bronze pitchers and a small bronze attachment in the form of a Silenus head. Soundings in the east corridor of the peristyle and in Room A along the north side indicate that the house was built in the mid-first century B.C. It continued to be occupied until the beginning of the fifth century A.D.[30]

Running along the north side of the House of the Bronze Head is a street, 26 m. long x 3.75 m. wide. On the north side of the street is a colonnade, 3 m. wide, supporting a portico along the front of the House of the Two Treasures. Only three of the four column bases of the portico remain in place. A fourth base, the second from the west end, was removed for the construction of a shallow rectangular lined pit of later date after the collapse of the colonnade. At its east end the street meets a street running south to north along the east side of the House of the Two Treasures. That street, outside the excavated area, is at a higher level reached by steps at the end of the colonnaded street. At its west end the colonnaded street meets a second south-north street along the west side of the House of the Two Treasures.

Taking advantage of the street, the excavators dug a deep sounding to bedrock along the entire north side of the House of the Bronze Head. At the bottom of the sounding over bedrock they found the remains of a circular post-Talayotic structure. Pottery found in the structure and immediately over bedrock was entirely hand-made indigenous ware. Between bedrock and a weak pavement of *sauló* (crushed and decomposing sandstone *marés*) was a fill, 0.40 m. deep, dating on the basis of the ceramic evidence to the second quarter of the first century B.C. The foundation footings of the House of the Bronze Head and the House of the Two Treasures were set in this fill. Seventy centimeters above the lower pavement was a second, harder pavement of *sauló* resting on a fill which the excavators date to the last quarter of the first century B.C. The pavement itself which was renewed at least twice is Augustan dating to the end of the first century B.C. or the early first century A.D. The fill over the upper pavement indicates that the street served as a thoroughfare until the middle of the third century A.D. when it fell into disuse and rubble from the House of the Bronze Head gathered over it.[31]

1.5.2 House of the Two Treasures

The insula north of the colonnaded street was occupied by two houses set back to back. The House of the Two

---

[29] The excavations are described in detail in two memoriae, A. Arribas, M. Tarradell, and D. Woods 1973 and A. Arribas, M. Tarradell, and D. Woods 1978a. Special studies of materials from the dig are included in A. Arribas ed. 1983c.

[30] For a detailed description of the House of the Bronze Head see Arribas 1973 and Arribas, 1978b: 161-189.
[31] Arribas 1978b: 189-207.

Treasures at the south end of the insula is the only one on the site completely excavated. It is an atrium house measuring 23 m. east to west x 19.40 m. south to north with a large room at the northwest corner extending the length on the west side to 22.50 m. The house takes its name from the discovery of two coin hoards, one of twelve coins in Room I dating to the mid-third century A.D. and the second of 21 coins in Room V dating to the end of the fourth century.[32]

The House of the Two Treasures contains ten rooms constructed around the atrium at the south side of the house. The main entrance is at the center of the south side through a vestibule (*fauces*) of two small rooms. The atrium is expansive, measuring 13.50 east to west x 12.50 m. north to south. At the center of the atrium is the *impluvium*, 6.30 x 3.30 m., with columns at its four corners. A small room at the southeast corner of the house was a shop with its entrance on the porticoed street. The spacious *triclinium,* 9.00 x 7.30 m., was located at the northwest corner of the house. A colonnaded portico ran along the entire south front of the house.

The excavators sank four soundings in order to date the construction of the house, one along the exterior of the west wall of the house, one in the *impluvium*, one beneath the floor in Room IV, and a fourth beneath the pavement in the *triclinium*. The ceramic evidence from the soundings indicates that the house was built in the reign of Augustus at the end of the first century B.C. or beginning of the first century A.D. It is also the case that when the house was constructed, its entrance was at the level of the Augustan pavement of the colonnaded street. The house suffered damage in the third quarter of the third century when the earlier coin hoard was deposited. Thereafter it was occupied perhaps by squatters until the beginning of the fifth century A.D. as the later coin hoard indicates.[33]

1.5.3 North House

Immediately north of the House of the Two Treasures in the same insula is a second house. The insula itself has been excavated to a distance of only 28.40 m. north to south so that only the southernmost rooms of the North House have been uncovered. It is estimated that the insula may be at least 40 m. long x 23 m. wide. The northern part has been destroyed by modern quarrying activity north of the Sa Portella property.

The excavated south section of the North House was divided in two by a substantial wall running south to north slightly east from the center of the north wall of Room V in the House of the Two Treasures. On either side of this main bearing wall there is a *taberna* or shop at the south end of the North House.

The entrance to the west shop is from the North-South street at the southwest corner of the house. It leads into a dog-leg corridor, 1.00 wide south to north x 5.80 m. long west to east. The corridor then turns north around a small rectangular room and widens to 2.00 west to east x 4.90 m. long south to north. The small room at the left of the entrance measures 3.20 south to north x 2.55 m. west to east. Off the north branch of the corridor lies the main room, 4.74 west to east x 8.30 m. south to north. Probably in the third century the southern part of the room was cut off by a coarse wall running from the main south-north wall of the building to the tip of the northwest corner of Room X of the House of the Two Treasures. This complex of corridors and rooms is clearly a shop with a small ante-room to the left of the main entrance. Pottery and coins from beneath the floors of the two rooms indicate that the shop was built in the Augustan period at the turn of the millennium.

The east shop is a complex of three rooms. The broad main entrance to the shop is from the street along the east side of the *insula* into a room, 3.70 east to west x 4.30 m. south to north, at the southeast corner of the North house. Behind this room to the west is another, 6.40 east to west x 4.30 m. south to north, with a wide doorway between the two rooms. There was a secondary door at the northwest corner of the room leading into the rear of the North House. The third room of the complex lies north of the first room and measures 3.70 east to west x 2.98 m. south to north. It is connected to the first room by a doorway at its southwest corner. This complex like the west shop was constructed in the reign of Augustus. Both shops were destroyed by fire at the beginning of the fifth century.[34]

1.5.4 North-South Street

Running north to south along the west side of the House of the Two Treasures is the North-South Street. It is 3.00 m. wide and has been excavated for a distance of 29 m. to its intersection with the Colonnaded Street. The street, however, may continue to the edge of the railroad station cutting, a distance of 40 m. In excavating the street to bedrock, the excavators identified three pavement surfaces, all of beaten earth. The lowest or earliest pavement was laid in the second quarter of the first century B.C. when the Northwest House was built. The second pavement, 0.20 m. above the first, dates early in the reign of Augustus when the House of the Two

---

[32] See Mattingly 1983: 248 and 269 for the coins and their significance. The third century hoard consists of *sestertii* only. The latest coin in the hoard is a *sestertius* of Decius Traianus, 249-251 A.D. The latest coin in the fourth century hoard is a bronze of Theodosius I dating to 393-395 A.D.
[33] Arribas 1978a: 9-108 and 1978b: 208-240. Mattingly 1983: 248 judges from the numismatic evidence that life continued at a subsistence level in the area of Sa Portella well into the fifth century.

[34] Arribas 1978b: 240-255 for a general description and Arribas 1978a: 109-146 for the pottery and other finds.

Treasures was constructed. The height of the street was adjusted to the level of the house. Finally in the Julio-Claudian period the level of the street was raised an additional 0.30 m.[35]

1.5.5 Northwest House

The Northwest House lies on the west side of the North-South Street opposite the House of the Two Treasures. Like the latter it is an atrium style house with its entrance on the North-South Street. The atrium seems to be located at the southeast corner of the house. It measures 10.00 north to south x 11.20 m. east to west. The *impluvium* with columns at the four corners and a low wall between the columns measures 3.00 north to south x 4.20 m. east to west. At the northeast corner of the atrium is a well. North of the atrium is a complex of five small rooms. The only access to these rooms from the atrium is through a narrow doorway immediately west of the well into the room at the southeast corner of the complex. Leaning along the west wall of this room and fallen into the beaten earth floor were large slabs of concrete pavement. The pavement slabs may have come from an upper floor, suggesting that the two rooms immediately north of the atrium were two stories high. The pottery evidence from beneath the floors of the complex indicates that the house was built in the second quarter of the first century B.C. It ceased to be used toward the middle of the third century A.D.[36]

North of the Northwest House are two *tabernae* or shops. Both are two rooms deep with wide doorways from the front room to the North-South Street. At some point the entrance to the south shop was closed by the construction of a wall running south to north in front of the doorway leaving a small gap at the northeast corner of the room for access. Both shops date to the middle of the first century B.C. They ceased to be occupied or used at the beginning of the second century A.D. It may have been at that time that the south shop was walled shut.[37]

South of the Northwest House is a complex of four or five rooms which have not been fully explored. There is a solid wall separating these rooms from the Northwest House. They do not seem to be part of the house.

It is of note that the earliest Roman structures, indeed, the earliest evidence of Roman settlement, in the area of Sa Portella date to the second quarter of the first century B.C., perhaps not before 70 B.C. The earliest buildings on the site are the House of the Bronze Head, the Northwest House, and the two shops north of the Northwest House. The two streets, the Colonnaded Street and the North-South Street, were laid out and paved when the houses were constructed. The House of the Two Treasures and the two shops north of that house date to the turn of the era in the reign of Augustus.

1.5.6 City Wall

The Northwest House was cut in two by the construction of a massive defensive wall running north to south for 50 m. along the entire west side of the property Sa Portella. The wall can be seen in section in both the north and south side of the railroad station cutting to the south of Sa Portella. It was constructed against the back wall of the two shops north of the Northwest House and at the rear of the impluvium of the house. The wall, thus, seems to run across the middle of the Northwest House, cutting off its west side. The wall is five meters wide. It is faced on the outside and inside with large marés blocks in regular courses up to nine courses high. The interior is filled with loose stones and rubble. The large exterior blocks, many cushioned ashlar, almost certainly come from major structures elsewhere in the city after they fell into disrepair. It has been difficult to date the wall as the excavations conducted in 1948-1949 along the outside of the wall were done without attention to stratigraphy. Probes into the interior of the wall during the excavations in Sa Portella were without significant results. The construction of the wall, however, may be related to the abandonment of the Northwest House in the mid-third century A.D. and to the collapse and abandonment of the Forum area and the rest of the city by the end of the third quarter of that century.

From 1962 to 1977 when it was thought that the wall encompassed the entire city, concerted attempts were made to trace it south of Sa Portella. In 1962 the excavators initiated probes with a proton magnetometer along the line of the wall in Camp d'en França and Ca'n Viver south of Sa Portella. Those probes did not succeed in locating the wall. From 1973 to 1976 excavations were conducted in Ca'n Viver and Ca'n Basser also without success in finding the wall. But in Ca'n Viver two significant covered drains or *cloacae* running perpendicular to the supposed line of city wall were excavated. Then in Camp d'en França in 1977 these efforts resulted in the discovery of a richly decorated house, the House of Polymnia, (Fig. 1.7) situated over the expected line of the wall. A hoard of 33 coins was found in the house, the latest of which was a *sestertius* of Trebonianus Gallus dating to 253 A.D. The house was destroyed by fire ca. 260 A.D. It thus appears that the Sa Portella wall was built in the last quarter of the third century in order to surround a small area at the northwest corner of the city to which the declining population of the city retreated during the economic troubles of the late third century.[38]

---

[35] Arribas 1978a: 217-230 for the ceramic evidence and dates.

[36] Arribas 1978a: 153-161 and Arribas 1978b: 257-262.

[37] Arribas 1978a: 147-153 and Arribas 1978b: 262-265 for a brief description the two shops along with analysis of the pottery and other evidence.

---

[38] For the city wall and the attempts to trace it south of Sa Portella see Arribas 1978b: 281-291. No published report

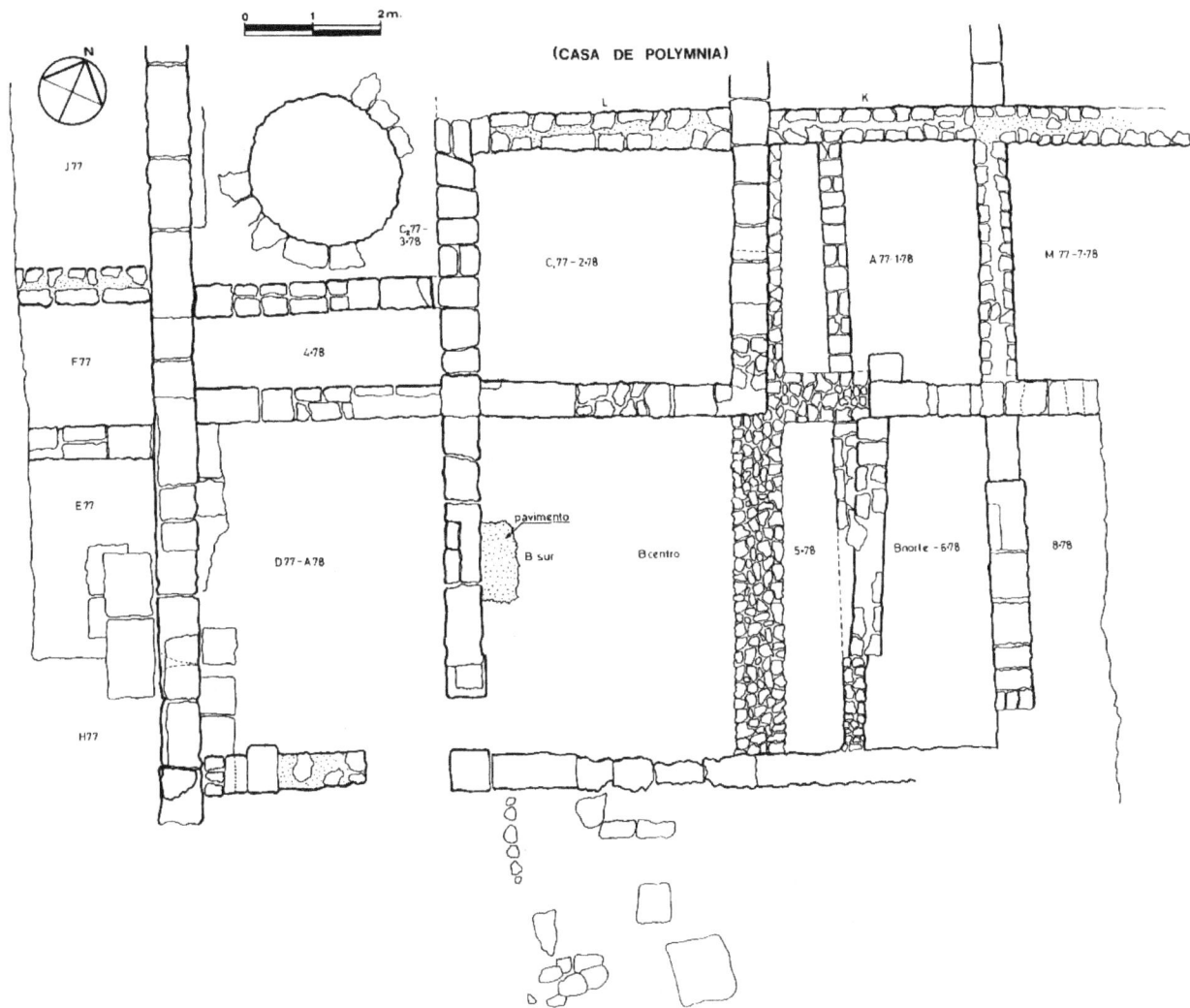

Fig. 1.7 The House of Polymnia in Camp d'en França.

1.6 The Size of Pollentia

Evidence from the excavations of Llabrés and Isasi, from Sa Portella, and from soundings made after 1962 make it possible to identify with some confidence the area occupied by the Roman city. To the north Pollentia extended certainly as far as the bypass street along the south side of modern Alcudia. Its eastern limit is marked by the road to the Roman theater. There is no sign of any Roman structure east of that road, only individual graves. On the south the ancient city extended no further than Ca'n Fanals south of the Roman theater and the chapel of Santa Ana where the ground level falls off and the Roman necropolis was excavated. On the west there is

now evidence of Roman house walls on the west side of the road past Santa Ana to the Puerto de Alcudia and Artá.

At a minimum the area of the Roman city measures 300 m. west to east x 600 m. north to south or 180,000 m^2 (= 18 hectares). These figures indicate that Pollentia was a substantial community occupying an intermediate position among Roman settlements in Spain. By comparison Barcino (Barcelona) was 13 ha. in area, Dertosa (Tortosa) 12 ha., Ilici (Elche) 12 ha., Lucentum (Alicante) 10-14 ha., Emporion (Ampurias) 21 ha., Tarraco (Tarragona) 70 ha., Augusta Emerita (Merida) 100 ha., Corduba 70 ha., and Caesar Augusta (Zaragoza) 50 ha.[39]

---

exists on the 1973-1977 excavations in Ca'n Viver and Camp d'en França or on the House of Polymnia, partially excavated 1977-1980. For the coin hoard from the House of Polymnia see H. B. Mattingly, below p. 60. See also Orfila 2000: 38-39 for the House of Polymnia and the soundings in Ca'n Basser.

---

[39] For the size of Roman settlements in Spain see M. Tarradell, 1978b: 320-321.

11

Pollentia was unwalled. For defense it relied on its location on an island and its distance from the sea, 1.5 klm. from the Bahía de Alcudia and 2.5 klm. from the Bahía de Pollença. Only at the end of the third century was a defensive wall built around the northwest corner of the city to which the people retreated. Similar contractions occurred in many cities along the east coast of Spain and elsewhere in the Roman Empire during this same period.[40]

1.7 Government Protection

In 1963 the Spanish government declared the entire area of the ancient city from Sa Portella in the north to the fields south of the chapel of Santa Ana a protected archaeological site. No construction may now take place in the fields over the Roman city. In 1973 the state began expropriating and buying individual fields. By 1995 eighteen properties on the site were purchased by the state. Only seven properties still remain in private hands.

---

[40] For the burst of wall-building and the contraction of communities at the end of the third century in Spain see S. J. Keay, 1988: 179-181. Along the northeast coast of Spain the walls of Gerunda, Barcino, and Caesaraugusta (Zaragoza) were rebuilt and strengthened toward the end of the third century. At Carthago Nova, Termes, and Conimbriga only a small section of the original city was walled for the first time. Contraction was a phenomenon in many parts of the Empire. Cf. the reduced size of Athens and the hasty construction of a defensive wall following the Herulian raid on the city in 267 A.D. See also Mattingly, below, p. 60.

Chapter 2

THE FORUM OF POLLENTIA

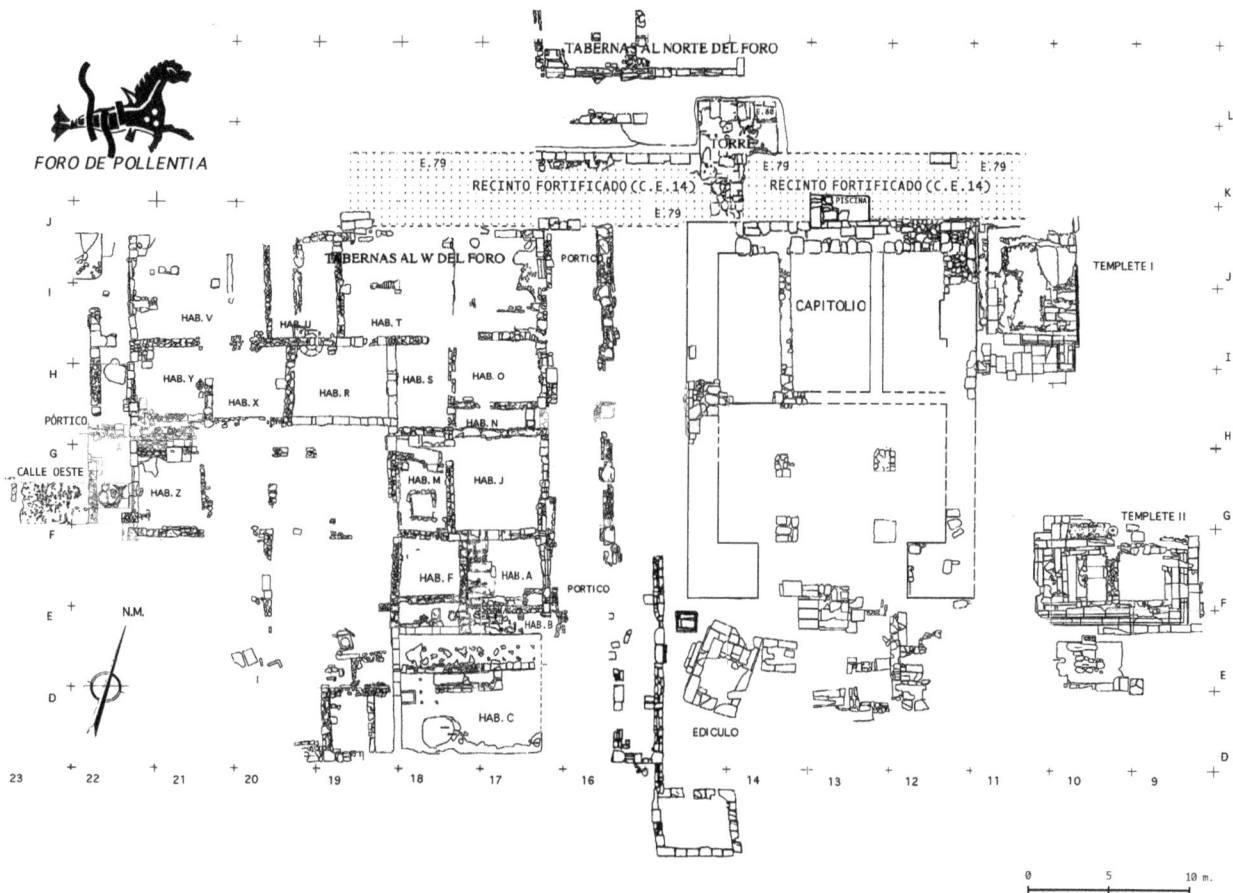

Fig. 2.1 Pollentia Forum

2.1 Overview

The effort to locate and excavate the Forum of Pollentia began in 1980 under the aegis of the Bryant Foundation. The excavators estimated the approximate location of the forum from the fact that the important honorific inscriptions found in the eighteenth and nineteenth centuries came from Camp d'en França as well as from the discoveries of Isasi in the same field. It was judged that Camp d'en França and specifically Ca'n Reinés in the southeast quadrant of that field were at or near the center of the Roman city. In the summer of 1980 the excavators sank a trench, 55 m. long, along the south side of Ca'n Reinés. Other trenches were then dug at a right angle north from the initial trench. It was almost immediately apparent to the excavators that they were digging in the area of the forum. In annual campaigns from 1980 to 1986 they exposed an area, 55 m. east to west x 40 m. south to north, at the north end of the forum and along its west side.

The Forum of Pollentia (Fig. 2.1) as well as the street grid of the city is oriented SSE to NNW with respect to the compass. The forum is closed at its north end by an impressive temple, the Capitolium, and a large monument base or temple at its northeast corner. Along its east side ten meters south of the monument base is a small temple at the southeast corner of the Capitolium. The rest of the east side north and south of the small temple remains unexcavated. On the west side are four *tabernae* or shops. Along the front of the shops ran a colonnaded portico. South of the shops and the colonnade on the west side is a large room with an *opus signinum* floor. The open area of the forum south of the Capitolium is 37 m. wide between the east front of the small temple and the colonnade. If the forum was laid out in accordance with the Vitruvian proportions of two to three, the length of the forum north to south may be estimated to be at least 55.5 m. In the open area immediately south from the southwest corner of the Capitolium is the temple's altar. It is the only structure in the city oriented with respect to the compass. At the two north corners of the altar stand two small monument bases. Probably in the mid-third century A.D. when buildings in the forum area were falling into disrepair the colonnade was walled up, and still later after the colonnade collapsed a coarse wall,

13

14 m. long, ending in a small rectangular room, 3.00 x 4.00 m., was constructed 2.40 m. east from the colonnade at its south end in front of the room with the *opus signinum* pavement.[1] Finally in the mid-fourth century A.D. when the forum had been abandoned more than two hundred graves were dug around the south, east, and north sides of the Capitolium. It is of interest that the area occupied by the Capitolium was respected. No graves have been found within its confines.

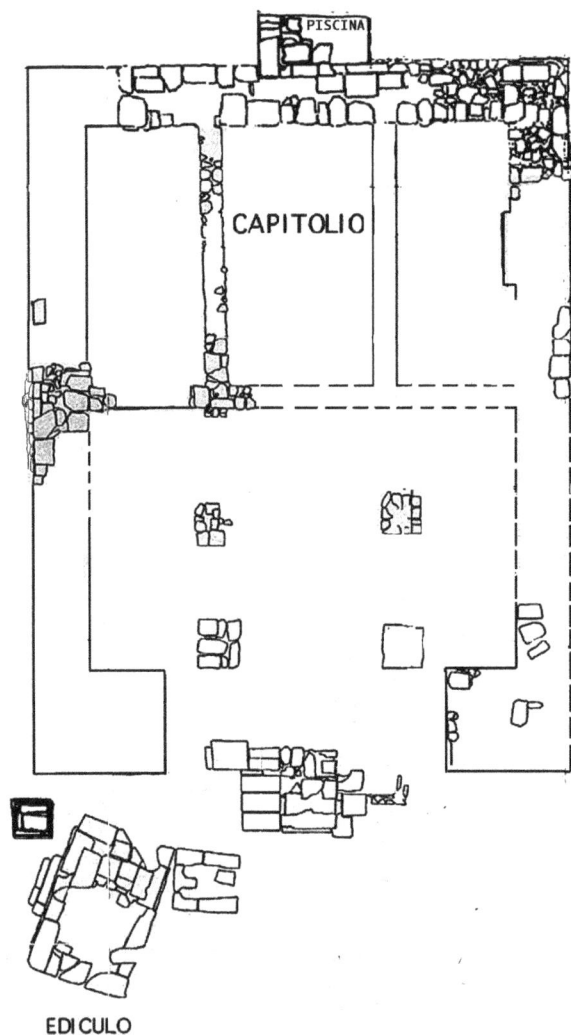

Fig. 2.2 The Capitolium

2.2 The Capitolium

It was not until 1985 that the excavators realized that the large structure at the north side of the forum was the Capitolium. Only the north wall of the podium, a small segment of the east podium wall at the northeast corner of

the building, another small section of the west podium wall, and parts of the cella walls survived the mining of the structure for building materials over the centuries. Nevertheless enough of the podium remains so that its overall dimensions and plan can be identified with reasonable confidence by tracing the line of the foundation trenches for the walls where the blocks themselves are missing. (Fig. 2.2) The bottoms of the trenches were filled with small stones to provide a level bedding for the sizable blocks of the walls. In preparation for constructing the temple the site was leveled by laying down a deep layer of sterile chalky earth (*blanquet*). After the podium walls were in place and the foundations of the cella walls and the four internal columns of the pronaos were laid, the entire area of the podium was filled with alternating layers of *blanquet* and field stones to the height of the temple floor. The fill was very compact, having almost the consistency of concrete.

The podium of the Capitolium measures 17.80 east to west x 23.30 m. north to south (=60.34 x 78.98 Roman feet). Because of the poor condition of the remaining walls it is not possible to determine the original height of the podium.[2] The exact outside dimensions of the temple itself are also not recoverable although its general plan may be reconstructed. The north wall of the podium is the best preserved feature of the building. It is 2.00 m. wide and has been preserved for a distance of 14.70 m. west from the northeast corner of the podium. It breaks off 3.10 m. east from the northwest corner. It is made up of two lines of large, somewhat irregular ashlar blocks set side by side and has been preserved to a maximum height of 1.80 m. Only one small section of the west wall survives, 10 m. south from the northwest corner of the podium. It is 2.00 m. wide and measures 3.90 m. north to south. A single block from the outer face of the wall remains in place 1.40 m. north of the preserved section. The rest of the wall has been traced by following the line of the foundation trench. North of the preserved section the bottom of the trench is filled with small leveling stones. But south of the section the leveling stones were missing, and the excavators were able to trace the trench only by removing the more lightly colored fill which collected in it when the large stones of the podium were removed. By careful excavation they succeeded in identifying the southwest corner of the podium. At the corner the wall turns east at a right angle for a distance of 4.00 m. The short south wall was widened to 3.50 m.

Similarly only a short section of the east wall of the podium, 4.00 m. long, has survived at the northeast corner of the building. The foundation trench of the east

---

[1] Two meters west of this late wall is another very poorly preserved wall of the same date. These walls seem to have enclosed three small rooms constructed south of the colonnade. See below pp. 58-59.

[2] Exact measurements of the Capitolium and other structures in the forum of Pollentia were made by Todd W. Parment in two visits to the site in 1995 and 1996. His study of the forum and the Capitolium was presented to the Department of Classics, Dartmouth College, as a senior honors thesis, *The Capitolium of Pollentia* (Hanover 1995). See also A. Arribas and M. Tarradell 1987: 126-127 and Orfila, Arribas, and Cau 1999: 108-109.

wall has not been carefully excavated. But the line of the wall can be traced by the identification of blocks from the wall which seem still to be in place. At a distance of 4.10 m. south from the preserved section at the northeast corner are four large blocks of the outer face of the wall certainly *in situ*. Three blocks from the inner face of the wall are visible 6.60 m. south of the four stones. At what must be the southeast corner of the podium there is a large block on end which seems to have been displaced from the corner. There symmetrically to the west wall the east wall turns west at a right angle for a distance of 4.00 m. At the northwest corner of this east wing of the south wall there is another large block still *in situ*. The position of these blocks confirms the general configuration of the south side of the podium. On that side there were two short spur walls, 3.50 wide, at the corners of the building. The open distance between the two spur walls at the center of the south side is 9.20 m.

The outer surfaces of the temple podium were stuccoed. A large fragment of stucco remains on the rear (north) wall of the podium behind a platform, 3.60 x 1.80 m., constructed against the north wall 7.40 m. west from the northwest corner of the podium. The façade of the platform was also stuccoed. It is not apparent what function the platform served.[3]

At the rear of the temple are three cellae. The fact that they are three in number identifies the temple as the Capitolium of Pollentia dedicated to the Capitoline triad of Jupiter, Juno, and Minerva. The central cella is the largest, measuring 5.00 east to west by 8.40 m. north to south. Only a line of leveling stones set in concrete marks the east wall of the cella. The west wall is better preserved. It is 0.70 m. wide, constructed with irregular marés blocks. Only two short sections of the south wall of the cellae have survived, one, 2.00 m. long, at the south end of the west wall and the other, 1.00 m. long, at the preserved section of the west podium wall. Both the east and west cellae are 3.70 m. wide from the inner face of the podium wall x. 8.40 m. deep. But it is likely that the two side cellae of the temple itself were, in fact, 4.50 m. wide. That measurement would center the east and west walls of the temple on the podium wall. If the outer walls of the cellae were 1.00 wide, the overall width of the temple may then be estimated to have been 17.40 m. It is significant that the south or front wall of the cellae is at the exact center of the long north-south axis of the temple. The overall dimensions of the Capitolium may thus be calculated to be 19.50 north to south x 17.40 m. west to east.[4]

At the center of the pronaos of the temple are four rectangular foundation bases for the interior columns at the front of the building. They are directly in line with the side walls of the middle cella. The bases are made up of marés blocks placed together in no set pattern. Only three of the bases have survived. The blocks from the fourth have been completely removed, but the cavity from which they were taken remains. The best preserved is the southwest base. It is rectangular, 1.60 north to south x 1.40 m. west to east. The south side of the base is positioned in line with the north side of the south wall of the podium, 1.00 m. east from its northeast corner or 3.40 m. east from the west face of the west podium wall. The southeast base, no blocks of which remain, was similarly positioned with respect to the east wing of the south podium wall. The distance between the two front column bases is 4.70 m.

The northwest column foundation is situated 2.50 m. north of the southwest base and 3.20 m. south from the front cella wall. It measures 1.40 north to south x 0.90 m. west to east. It is apparent, however, that blocks have been removed from its west side so that it may originally have been roughly square. The northeast base is square, 1.40 m. on each side. It is positioned 4.70 m. east from the northwest base, but strangely it is not in line with the northwest base but is 0.50 m. north of it or 3.00 m. north from the southeast base. This discrepancy may have resulted from poor planning on the part of the builders. It is also possible that stones have been removed from the south side of the northeast base.

At roughly the middle of the south side of the podium is a rectangular platform, 3.10 west to east x 2.80 m. south to north. Along the west side of the platform are five finely cut large blocks, three of them measuring 1.30 x 0.60 m. The blocks on the east side measure 1.80 m. in length and are much less well preserved. The south side of the lowest block on the east side is heavily eroded or worn so that it is now convex in shape. The platform projects 1.80 m. south from the line of the south podium wall. The excavators have suggested that the platform was the base for stairs leading to the pronaos of the temple. It should be noted, however, that the platform is not centered on the north-south axis of the temple but is located 0.50 m. west of center. There is some evidence on the ground that stones have been removed from the east side of the platform. Certainly at a later date a marble base 0.78 x 0.69 m. was taken from the west end of the large *opus signinum* floor on the west side of the forum and placed at the east side of the platform. Blocks at the east side of the platform were cut away to receive the marble base. But even if the possibility is taken into account that blocks from the east side of the platform were removed, the position of the supposed steps remains off center. The eroded or worn edge of the lowest block

---

[3] The platform, probably a shallow rectangular basin with an *opus signinum* bottom, is not on the earlier site plan. Just at its west side but not part of the platform is a pilaster base or capital which may have come from one of the antae of the Capitolium. For the platform see Parment 1995: 20 and Orfila, Arribas, and Cau 1999: 110. Such basins attached to temples date to the reign of Augustus.

[4] The Vitruvian cannons for a Roman temple dictate that the cella should occupy the inner half of the building or that the

cella and the pronaos of a temple should be equally deep. The Pollentia Capitolium measures 66 x 59 Roman feet (@ 1 ft. Roman = 0.295 m.).

on the east side of the platform also does not fit the pattern for steps. The edge is convex in shape, not concave as is to be expected if it had served as a step. There are traces of stucco on the well-preserved west side of the platform. This stucco as well as the general configuration of the structure suggests that it was a monument base or an altar set into the line of steps leading to the temple and filling the space between the two central columns of the pronaos.[5] The actual steps to the temple may have occupied the wide gap between the wings of the south podium wall.

The remains of the Capitolium, frustratingly lamentable as they are, indicate with some certainty that it was a tetrastyle prostyle Italic or Tuscan temple. It had four columns across the front with in all probability two columns in antis behind. The nearest Italian analogue in plan is the Capitolium at Cosa dating to the mid-second century B.C.[6] It is possible but not probable that there were two rows of four columns across the pronaos at Pollentia, but the general crudeness of construction techniques at Pollentia makes this more sophisticated option less likely. The distance between the two central columns across the front of the temple was 5.00 m. The two outer columns were set 4.50 m. from the inner columns. Two column drums, 0.90 m. in diameter, were built into the late wall at the southwest corner of the forum. In all likelihood they came from the Capitolium after its collapse. If so, the columns of the pronaos may be estimated to have been 6.30 m. high.[7] The outer walls of the cella, it has been suggested, were at least one meter thick. They were set a few centimeters in from the outer edge of the podium. As was the case with all other walls on the site, the temple walls were probably constructed with a low sill of sandstone blocks with mud bricks above. The architrave and roof of the temple were of wood. The outside and inside of all walls would have been covered with stucco. In spite of its relatively crude construction the Capitolium was without question the most impressive structure in Pollentia.

In the summer of 1995 an attempt was made to date the construction of the Capitolium. Unfortunately in the early years of the excavations the excavators gave inadequate attention to floor levels, and the ceramic evidence collected has not yet been analyzed. But in 1995 Parment, supervised by Doenges, dug four soundings in the area of the temple. In one of them at the south end of the surviving section of the west podium wall he excavated a small patch of pavement of largish marés stones laid directly over *blanquet* at depth 2.25 against the west face of the wall.[8] From the pavement he recovered eight fragments of *terra sigillata Arretina*, four fragments of fine wall pottery, and nineteen fragments of Roman common pottery. This pottery evidence suggests that the Capitolium was built during the reign of Augustus at the turn of the era. In another sounding in the center cella of the temple 2.10 m. south from the north podium wall he found in three strata of reddish earth over *blanquet* 27 fragments of hand-made Talayotic pottery, one fragment of an Ebusitan amphora, and three fragments of coarse common pottery either Iberian or Roman. One of the Talayotic fragments from the upper stratum is the bottom of a Talayotic crested cup. These cups are commonly found on Talayotic sanctuary sites. The evidence from this sounding suggests that the Capitolium was built directly over a post-Talayotic sanctuary still functioning in the first century B.C.

The date of the dismantling and collapse of the temple is equally problematic. Only three coins were found in fill over the Capitolium, a Republican As, an As of Commodus dating to 191-192 A.D., and an As of Gordian III dating 238-244 A.D.[9] By the end of the third century the structure was in grave disrepair. Parts of the building, however, may have survived into the fifth century.

2.3 Northeast Temple or Monument

At the northeast corner of the Capitolium is a sizable rectangular structure, 7.20 north to south x 5.70 m. west to east. (Fig. 2.3) The excavators identified it as a temple, but certain features of the structure make that judgment suspect. At its southeast corner there is a low rectangular projection, 1.60 x 1.10 m. There may have been a similar projection at the southwest corner, but all building blocks from that corner have been robbed. Two blocks of the lowest course at the south front of the structure have a torus molding at the bottom. This molding is then carried around the southeast projection. These decorative blocks seem to preclude the hypothesis that there were steps between the projections. Four blocks *in situ* along the west side are cushioned ashlar blocks. The lowest course along the east side of the structure is also of cushioned ashlar construction. It is possible that the sides of the structure sloped inward so that it measured only 6.30 x 4.20 m. at the top.[10] The

---

[5] For a similar platform or altar built into the steps note the Temple of Mars Ultor in the Forum of Augustus in Rome.
[6] On the Capitolium at Cosa see F. Brown, *Cosa: The Making of a Roman Town* 1980: 51-56 and Parment 1995: 26.
[7] According to Vitruvius, *De architectura* 4.7.2, the height of a column should be seven times its diameter at the base. In the summer of 1995 a quarter of an Ionic or Corinthian fluted column drum was found along the line of the late Roman wall of the colonnade west of the Capitolium. The diameter of the drum is 0.70 m. Vitruvius recommends that a Corinthian column should be tapered at its top to a diameter three-quarters the diameter of the base. If columns of the Capitolium were 0.90 in diameter at the bottom, the fluted drum would meet roughly the Vitruvian standard. It is likely that the Capitolium columns were unfluted at the bottom while at the top they were fluted and tapered. It is unfortunate that no column capital or base has been found on the site.

[8] The sounding measured 0.50 x 0.50 m. at the south side of grid square H-15.
[9] H. B. Mattingly below pp. 67-69.
[10] A suggestion by Parment 1995. For this structure and the East Temple see Orfila, Arribas, and Cau 1999: 110-111.

structure has survived to a height of only 0.75 m. There is no indication of interior walls. The center of the structure, indeed, is filled with a mixture of *blanquet*, earth, and stones. The excavators estimate that it was in a state of disrepair and already partially dismantled by the end of the first century A.D. It is curious that the structure stands so close to the Capitolium, just 0.50 m. east from the temple. An indication perhaps of its importance is the fact that the area at the front of the structure between the projections is paved with large rectangular marés stones in no identifiable pattern.

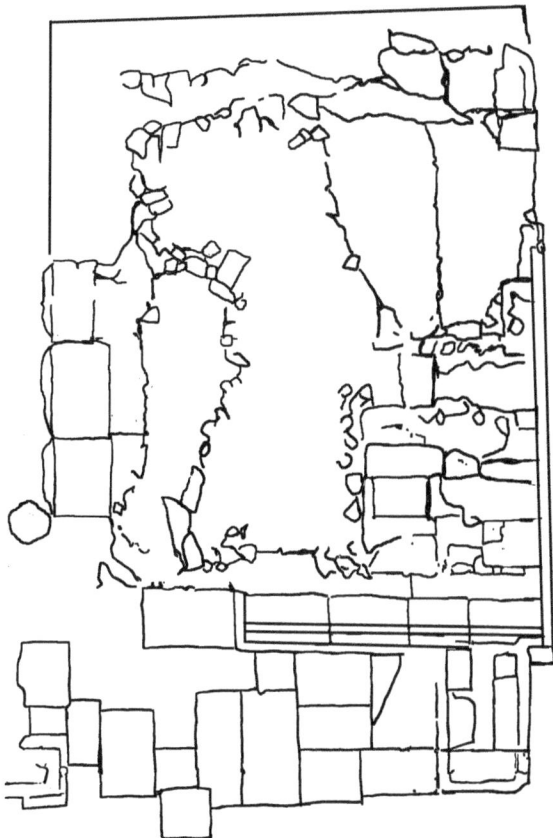

Fig. 2.3 The Northeast Temple or Monument

On the pavement in front of the structure the excavators found two fragments of a dedicatory inscription, 1.25 x 0.54 m. One of the fragments had been reused as a side of a cist grave. The inscription is in two lines, the upper in block letters 0.10 m. high and the lower in letters 0.07 m. high. The inscription reads,

. . .[A]UG LEG PRO PR F C
. . .[P]RO LEG DEDICAVIT.

Also found in fill in front of the structure was a decorative crowning member or balustrade of marés, 1.20 long x 0.55 tall x 0.09 m. thick, in a leaf or flower design. The design consists of two types of leaves or fronds which alternate. Whether this decorative architectural

piece comes from the structure, from the Capitolium, or from another building needs further study.[11]

The general design of this structure at the side of the Capitolium seems to suggest that it was the base of a major monument, not a temple. Its size suggests that it may have held an equestrian statue. The life-size bronze head of a horse found by Isasi in 1923 in fill near the chapel of Santa Ana (p. 00) indicates that there was an equestrian statue in the city of Pollentia. The only structure found thus far in the forum which is of a size to accommodate such a statue is this one at the northeast corner of the Capitolium.

On the pavement in front of the monument exactly covering the space between it and the Capitolium is a small statue base, 0.70 west to east x 0.50 m. north to south. Stones from the north side of the base, however, have been removed so that the base originally was rectangular, 0.70 x 1.35 m. The statue base, indeed, would have fit nicely between the temple and a missing west projection on the front of the monument. It is difficult not to conclude that the statue was purposely placed in this position to hide the narrow gap between the two structures.

2.4 East temple

Ten and a half meters south from the monument base on the east side of the forum is a small rectangular building, 10.10 west to east x 6.40 m. north to south. (Fig. 2.4) It is of interest that this building stands just 4.00 m. directly east from the southeast corner of the Capitolium. Most of the building blocks of the structure have been robbed so that only the lowest foundation course remains. Along the south and east sides of the building there is a stone gutter to catch runoff from the roof. All but three blocks at the northwest corner are missing from the north side of the building. A wall, three courses high, runs north to south at the center of the building. The wall seems to divide the building into two square rooms, each 4.00 x 4.00 m., although the internal features of the building need further study.

The excavators identify the building as a small temple. If they are correct, it may have had two columns in antis at the east front and a single cella at the rear. It is somewhat awkward that it is located so close to the Capitolium rather than further south with its entrance on the open area of the forum. Its position makes it almost certain that it faced east and that the east side of the forum has not yet been identified.

No date has thus far been assigned to the temple. An examination of the building conducted in 2001 revealed that much of the material used in its construction came from other structures. The temple seems to be post-Augustan, but how late remains to be determined.

---

[11] On the inscription and crest see A. Arribas and M. Tarradell 1987: 127.

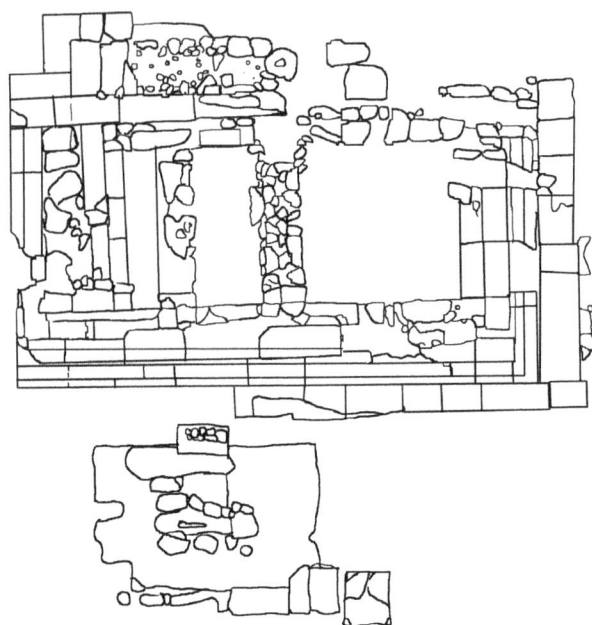

Fig. 2.4 The East Temple or Temple II

There are indications on the ground that there was a small rectangular room, 4.00 east to west x 2.60 m. south to north, abutting the temple at its southwest corner. The room, however, has not been fully excavated.

2.5 Open Area of the Forum

The open area of the forum south of the Capitolium seems to have been paved originally with small flat stones set in clay. Patches of this pavement may be seen south of the monument base at the front steps of the temple. Later, perhaps in the second century, a thick (0.10 m.) macadam-like pavement of small stones in dark mortar was laid. Remains of it can be seen along the west side of the forum and at the base of the free standing monuments. The excavators unfortunately did not pay sufficient attention to preserving pavement levels.

Just 1.50 m. south from the southwest corner of the Capitolium is a large rectangular base, 5.40 south to north x 3.50 west to east. It still stands 0.60 m. high in three ashlar courses. The presence of cuttings in the blocks of the third course to hold metal clamps indicates that the monument was originally at least four courses high. At the center of the west side of the base are what seem to be two shallow steps, 2.00 m. long. This base is the only structure in the Pollentia forum which is oriented with respect to the compass. The excavators originally proposed that the base served as a speaker's platform at one side of the temple. But its orientation to the points of the compass makes it highly likely that the monument was the ancient altar of the city. If so, it would be the oldest structure in the forum. A priest standing on the steps at the altar faced the rising sun. For similar altars set at an angle to their temples but oriented to the points

of the compass compare the *Ara della Regina* at Tarquinia and the altar of the Capitolium at Cosa.[12]

One meter west from the northwest corner of the altar is a small statue base, 1.30 west to east x 1.20 m. south to north at the bottom and 0.90 m.[2] above. The monument is four courses high. Each course is made up of two large blocks the direction of which alternates in successive courses. At some point the top course was removed and then put back in the wrong direction. There is a torus molding around the bottom of the base except on the north side which is flat. The implication is that the monument was to be viewed from the south, indeed, from the steps of the altar. It may also be that the base was once placed against a wall but was then moved to the spot it now occupies.[13]

At the northeast corner of the altar is what seems to be another statue base, 2.10 west to east x 2.00 m. south to north. Only its lowest course has survived. The center blocks of the base were dug out to accommodate two late Roman graves. Similarly two late graves were dug into the top course of the altar.

Only 1.20 m. west from the southwest corner of the altar is a late wall, 14.00 m. long ending in a small room, 4.00 x 3.00 m. projecting east from the wall at its south end. The wall is very poorly constructed from reused blocks and stones. It seems to have been the east wall of a series of three narrow rooms. The south room of the three measures 3.00 south to north x 2.00 m. west to east, and the central room 5.40 south to north.[14] Only one block between the central room and the north room remains in place. Not enough of the north room remains to measure it. The entrance to this complex was at the center of the central room facing the altar. The wall and the room seem to date to the end of the third century or later.

2.6 West Side of the Forum

Along the west side of the forum opposite to the Capitolium are four *tabernae* or shops. (Fig. 2.5) In front of the shops is a colonnade or portico, preserved for a distance of 21 m. north to south. The colonnade stands 3.20 m. east from the front of the shops and 4.50 m. west from the Capitolium. Six column footings, 0.90 m.[2], are still in place. A seventh footing at the south end of the colonnade is missing. With a seventh column the colonnade would have been 24 m. long. The footings are each 3.00 m. apart. Each has a circular cutting, 0.60 m. in diameter, for receiving the base of its column. There is no evidence on the ground that the colonnade ran past the front of the southernmost shop.

---

[12] Brown 1980 and Parment 1995: 31-32. For doubts about the early date of the altar which rests on a second century AD surface see below p. 58.
[13] Parment 1995: 5-6.
[14] The middle room of this complex was partially excavated in 2000. See below, pp. 58-59.

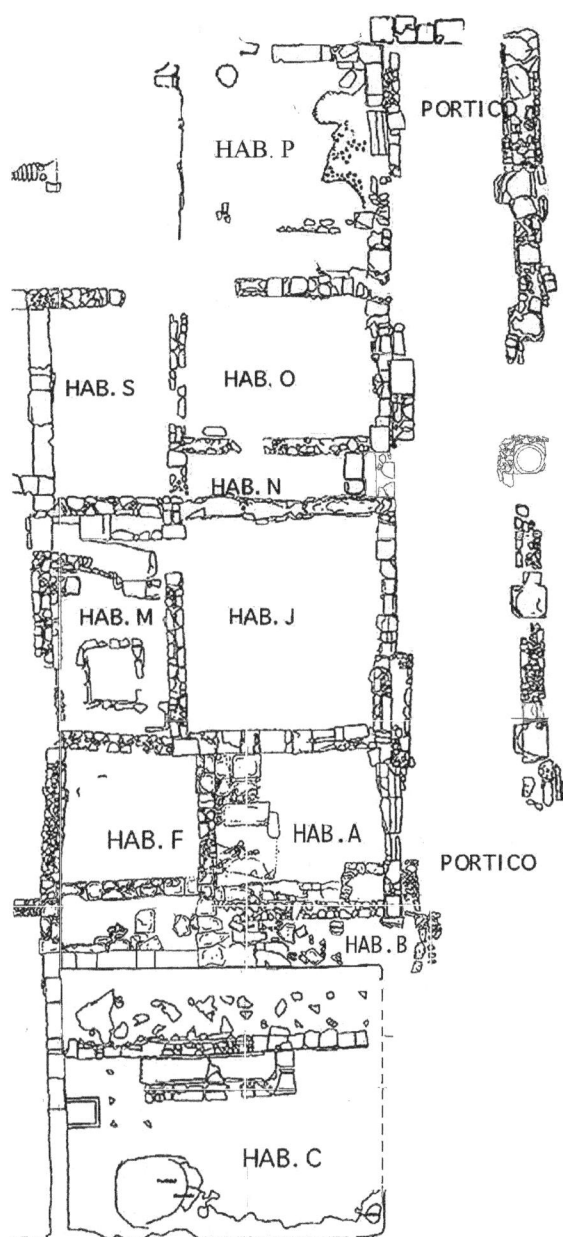

Fig. 2.5 Shops along the west side of the Forum

In the early to mid-third century the colonnade was walled up, converting the colonnade into an enclosed gallery. The wall between the columns was constructed from reused building stones taken from other structures.

The northernmost of the four shops (Room P) is the most poorly preserved. Only the front wall and parts of the north and south walls have survived. The line of the west wall can be traced only from its shallow foundation trench. The shop measures 4.25 north to south x 5.25 m. east to west. It faces the colonnade and is entered by way of a doorway, 2.80 m. wide. In the entrance threshold there is a narrow channel to receive a wooden closure. The north and south walls are preserved for a distance of

only 3.00 m. A sizable area of pebble pavement remains along the east side of the room.

The shop may have had a narrow back room to the west, but only a section of its south wall, 2.00 m. long, remains. Because the east wall of the room is entirely missing, it is not possible to determine whether there was a doorway between it and the shop. There may have been an entrance from the north as well.

Along the south side of the shop there is a narrow corridor, 1.00 wide. Whether it served as a pantry/storeroom or held a staircase cannot be known for lack of evidence on the ground. There is, however, no entrance to the corridor from the portico.

Just at the east side of the portico in front of this shop an iron window grate was found in 1985. The grate measures 1.35 x 1.00 m. and is made up of five horizontal iron bars and five vertical bars. At the intersection of the bars are spiked stars. The lower left quarter of the grate is missing. The grate may have come from a large upper window over the doorway of the shop.[15]

The next shop to the south (Room O) measures 4.00 north to south x 5.30 m. east to west. Its doorway facing the colonnade is 3.00 m. wide. The threshold lacks the normal channel for holding a wooden closure. In the early third century a low stone bench, 2.20 m. long, was set in front of the entrance perhaps for displaying goods from the shop. The west wall of the room has been preserved for a distance of only 3.40 m., the north wall for a distance of 3.80 m. so that the northwest corner of the room is missing. This shop seems to have had no rear room.

South of Room O and between the two shops to the north and the two to the south is another narrow corridor (Room N), 1.20 wide x 5.58 m. long east to west. It is entered from the colonnade, but its doorway is set back 0.75 m. from the front wall of the shops. It is closed at its west end. The corridor almost certainly housed a wooden staircase, evidence that the shops on the west side of the forum were two-stories high.

Behind the second shop and the stairway is another room (Room S), 5.45 south to north x 3.15 m. east to west. The west wall of the room which separates it from Room R in the Dartmouth sector is not quite parallel to the east wall so that the room is not a perfect rectangle. This wall is properly the east wall of Room R and dates along with Room R to the end of the first century B.C. or the beginning of the first century A.D. There is no doorway

---

15 For the grate see A. Arribas, 1993. A similar grate but without the stars at the intersection of the bars was found intact on the north side of Room Y in the Dartmouth sector. See below, p. 29. Such grates have been rarely found outside Pompeii and Herculaneum. It is, therefore, exceptional that two were found so close together at Pollentia.

from the second shop into this room. The entrance to the room was perhaps at its missing northeast corner into the room west of the first shop. The two rooms may have been an independent complex with its entrance to the north.

The next shop (Room J) immediately south of the stairway is the largest of the four, measuring 5.35 east to west x 5.75 m. north to south. It has a wide (2.60 m.) doorway with a channeled threshold opening onto the portico. The doorway is slightly off-center to the north. There is a second doorway at the northwest corner of the shop, leading into a short corridor, 3.00 east to west x 1.80 m. north to south, and from it to a rear room (Room M), 3.90 north to south x 3.10 m. east to west. The main feature of this rear room is a deep stone-lined rubbish pit or *pozo negro*, trapezoidal in shape, toward its south side. The pit measures 1.25 m. east to west x 1.33 along its west wall and 1.56 along its east wall south to north. The walls of the pit are strikingly well-built in regular ashlar construction as compared to normal shop and house walls in Pollentia. From the pit a large number of ceramic canteens were recovered. They and other vases dating to the end of the second century were evidently thrown into the pit to fill it when it ceased to be used. In the shop (Room J) the excavators found a complete set of stone balance weights.

The last or southernmost shop (Room A) is the best preserved, measuring 4.10 north to south x 4.50 m. east to west. It has a wide entrance, 2.60 m. in length, with a channeled threshold. At the southeast corner of the shop just to the left of the doorway is a platform or counter, 1.06 x 0.93 m. Room A was investigated in depth from 1996 to 1998.[16] In the third century a doorway at the northwest corner of the room led to Room F which served as an added backroom to the shop. Room F measures 3.92 north to south x 3.64 m. east to west, but its shape is irregular. Its west wall is not quite parallel to the east wall, nor is the north wall parallel to the south wall. The east wall, the height of which was raised in a third century reconstruction, is properly the west wall of Room A. The south wall butts up against the east wall and is not bonded to it. Similarly the west wall of the room butts up against the south wall of Room M which angles in a west-northwesterly direction. Hence Room F appears to be a third-century addition the shop.

South of the four shops is a narrow passageway or corridor (Room B), 1.20 wide x 9.20 m. long east to west. The passage is open at its east end but seems to have been closed in the third century at its west end by a wall which is only partially preserved.[17] South of the passage is a large rectangular *opus signinum* pavement (Room C) measuring 7.45 north to south x 8.30 m. east to west. If there were once walls around the pavement, none remains

except for five blocks along the west side just below the level of the pavement. There is some evidence from excavation at deeper levels in 1996, 1997, and 2001 that similar blocks were removed along the north and east sides of the pavement. At the center of the west side of the pavement is a rectangular imprint, 0.78 x 0.69, left after the removal of the statue base which was then placed at the east side of the platform at the center of the Capitolium steps. The excavators have proposed that the pavement is the floor of either a large cult building or the *curia* of Pollentia. Directly in front of the entrance stood the city altar. Beyond the altar were the steps leading up to the Capitolium. The pavement is at the same level as the floor of the forum in front of the temple. Late walls at its west end remain to be investigated.

Near its southwest corner the *opus signinum* pavement of Room C has collapsed over a deep pit, 1.30 m. in diameter at the top and 2.00 m. at the bottom. The pit is 3.00 m. deep. The excavators describe it as a well, but it may have been a rubbish pit for the disposal of broken or discarded material. The pit was sealed with layers of clay when the pavement was put down. Pottery in the pit was predominantly Campanian A, B, and C wares, fine wall pottery, and Roman common pottery dating to the middle of the first century B.C. On the evidence of materials from the pit the pavement, therefore, may be dated no earlier than the mid-first century B.C.[18]

At some point a rough wall, 8.00 m. long, running west to east was built on top of the *opus signinum* pavement 1.80 m. south from its north side. At the center of the south side of the wall is a shallow basin, 3.60 x 0.60 m., lined with cement. It may have served as a watering or feeding trough for animals. The date of the wall and basin has not been determined.

Twelve meters west of the third shop (Room J) along the west side of the forum is a shop (Room Z) excavated from 1994 to 1999. It faces the West Street south of Room Y and a narrow passageway between the two shops. Room Z measures 4.60 north to south x 3.90 m. east to west. Its entrance, 2.86 m. wide, has a channeled threshold for holding a wooden closure.[19]

2.7 Inscriptions

In the early years of the Forum excavation numerous fragments of inscriptions were recovered. Most of the

---

[16] For a full description of Room A and its history see below pp.55-56.
[17] For Room B see below p. 56.

---

[18] Equip 1993: 227-243. Excavation at the lowest levels in Room B in 1998 revealed the foundation of a wall running south through Room B and under the *opus signinum* pavement of Room C along the line of the west wall of Room A. The excavators propose that the area beneath Room C in the second quarter of the first century B.C. was divided into two rooms.
[19] For a detailed description of Room Z and its history see below pp. 50-52.

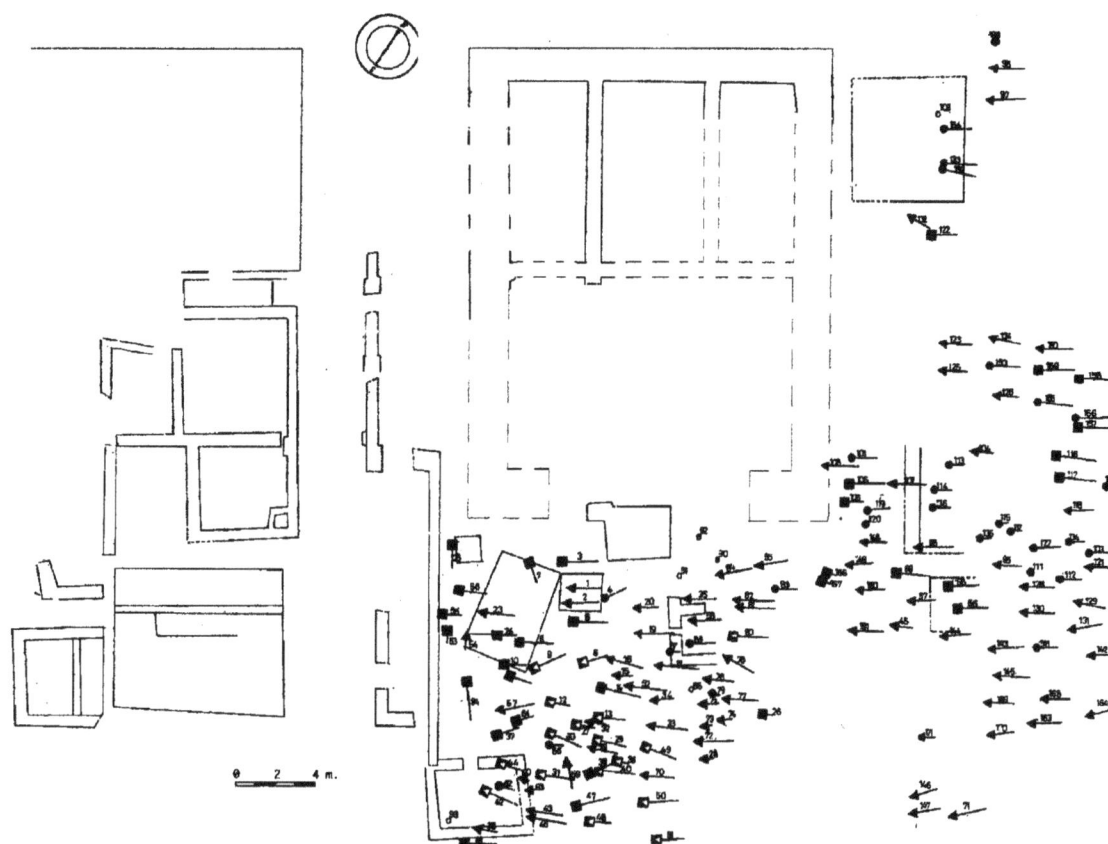

Fig. 2.6 The Forum Necropolis

fragments are of thin (rarely more than three centimeters thick) plaques of marble or fine local limestone suitable for attachment to a pedestal or monument. All but one of the inscriptions appear to be dedicatory to imperial officials or local dignitaries. The earliest inscription which reads IULI PR[onepos] in block letters 15.8 m. high may have come from a dedication to the elder Drusus, brother of the Emperor Tiberius. Most of them seem to refer to emperors of the second century such as Marcus Verus and the Severi. One of the latest makes possible mention of Licinius and Galienus. The most surprising feature of the inscriptions found in the forum is their fragmentary condition. More than thirty fragments, for instance, were found of the inscription to Drusus. Nearly all of the fragments are very small, too broken for restoration. Most of them were found in a limited area in front of the colonnaded portico. These facts suggest that the inscriptions were purposely smashed and discarded. The circumstance under which that action occurred may be related to the end of public life in the forum.[20]

2.8 Final Phases

Public activity in the forum came to an end with the firing of the shops on the west side of the square. Over the latest floors there was a thick layer of ashes, burnt mud brick, roof tiles, and rubble. Many marble

inscription fragments were burnt black by fire. It is significant, however, that there was no sign of fire in the Capitolium. It is possible that the temple had fallen into disrepair and had been partly dismantled before the shops were burned. But parts of the building may have survived into the fourth century. Not a single late grave was dug over the area occupied by the Capitolium. The date of the final abandonment of the forum area is signaled by the numismatic evidence. The continuous coin record from the forum breaks off with a reform coin of Tacitus dating 275-276 A.D. and three reform coins of Probus, 276-282 A.D. There follows a gap of twenty-five years. The record resumes in the early fourth century with seven coins of Maxentius and Constantine followed by a four coins of Constantius II, 341-348 A.D., and four coins in all of Valens, 364-378 A.D., Valentinian, 378-383 A.D, and Theodosius I, 383-387 A.D. These later coins are found in fill associated with the forum necropolis.[21]

2.9 Forum Necropolis

Around the south, east, and north sides of the Capitolium more than two hundred graves have been excavated. (Fig. 2.6) They are of three types: simple *fossa* graves at times dug directly into the tops of earlier walls and monuments, cist graves lined with thin slabs of marés with or without

---

[20] A. Arribas and M. Tarradell 1987: 130-133.

[21] H. B. Mattingly below p. 69.

cover slabs, or cist graves with a stone bench or mound above them marking the location of the grave. The body was invariably laid out in a supine position with (except for a single grave) the head to the west and the feet to the east. In only a very few graves was there any offering. There is no indication of the use of a wooden casket. The corpse was wrapped in a simple shroud and placed directly in the ground. From the numismatic evidence the graves date from the early to the mid-fourth century A.D., barely fifty years after the abandonment of the forum. In one grave there was a worn bronze of Probus, in another a follis of Constantine, and in a late cist grave a second follis of Constantine. There is no evidence that burials in the Forum necropolis continued into the early fifth century when those still living in the small enclave at Sa Portella left the city.[22]

2.10 North of the Capitolium

One meter north of the northwest corner of the Capitolium is a massive platform or tower, 5.00 x 4.80 m., constructed out of reused building blocks. Running west from the platform is a well built wall of large finely-cut reused marés blocks in a single line which has been traced westward for some ten meters. It is possible that there was a corresponding wall on the east side of the platform, but unfortunately evidence of it has been destroyed. Investigation from 1997 to 1999 has revealed that the platform and wall are parts of a massive fortification system along the north side of the forum area.[23]

Northwest from the defensive tower are two large rooms, only one of which (Room 01) has been excavated. It measures, 5.75 east to west x 5.10 m. south to north. The west wall of the room is not quite parallel to the east wall. The entrance is to the south through a doorway, 3.00 m. wide, with a channeled threshold. To the left of the entrance is a built platform or counter, 1.30 x 1.25 m. A similar platform, 1.20 x 0.80 m., is located at the southeast corner of the room. Centered on the doorway 1.60 m. north from the entrance is a freestanding column, 0.60 m. in diameter, on a low base. At the northeast corner of the room is a circular pit, 1.20 m. in diameter. The room almost certainly was a shop. Found in it was a small bronze figurine of a bull. (Fig. 2.7) Like the shops in the forum it was destroyed by fire in the third quarter of the third century A.D.[24] East of this shop is another room (Room 02), 5.60 m. west to east x 5.10 north to south. Only the tops of its walls have been exposed. The excavators date the construction of both rooms to the early second century A.D. The two rooms faced a portico and a wide street running east to west north of the Capitolium and the shops on the west side of the forum.

Fig 2.7 Bronze bull figurine found in Room 01 north of the Capitolium

---

[22] On the late necropolis see A. Arribas and M. Tarradell 1987: 135-136. For a list of other burial grounds on the site and their location see Orfila, Arribas, and Cau 1999: 100 and Fig. 1.2 above.
[23] For the late fortification system see below pp. 57-58.

---

[24] This room was excavated in 1992 as part of a program to extend the excavations north of the forum. The effort did not continue beyond that year.

Chapter 3

DARTMOUTH COLLEGE SECTOR

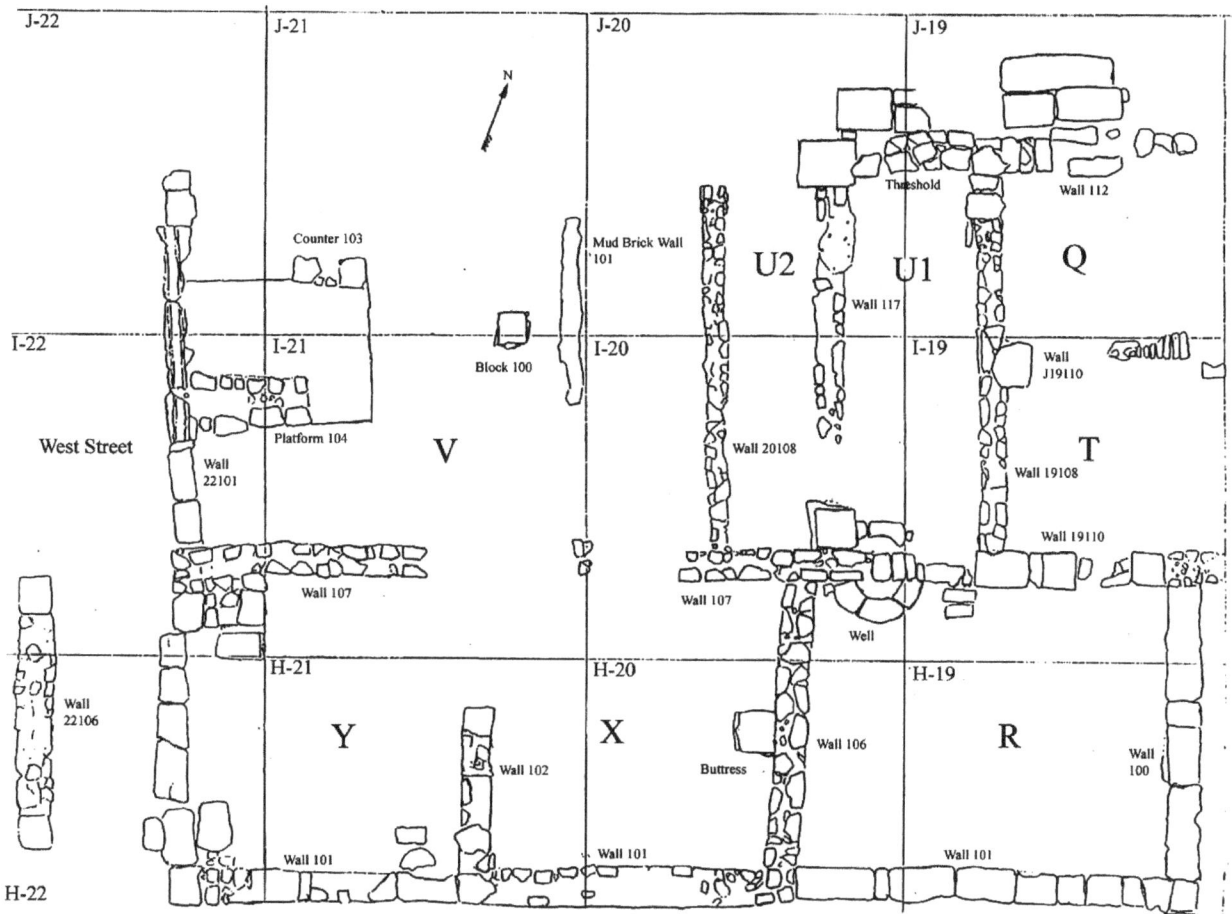

Fig. 3.1 Bryant Foundation-Dartmouth College Sector

3.1 Dartmouth College Excavations

The Bryant Foundation-Dartmouth College sector of the excavations on the site of Roman Pollentia is located northwest of the open area of the Forum roughly eighteen meters west from the Capitolium. It encompasses squares H-19 to 22, I-19 to 22, and J-19 to 22 on the general grid of the Forum excavations.

Excavation in the sector began in the summer of 1986. Campaigns were conducted from the first week in July through mid-August annually until 1993. In 1995 and 1997 soundings were excavated in Rooms V, Y, and X to gather data about the early history of the site. The excavations were undertaken with the generous support of the William L. Bryant Foundation of South Woodstock, Vermont, under the auspices of the Department of Classics, Dartmouth College, Hanover, New Hampshire. Each summer four Bryant Foundation Archaeological Interns, undergraduate students at Dartmouth College selected by the Department of Classics, participated in the excavations. From 1986 to 1995 thirty-nine Bryant Foundation Interns were active in the Dartmouth sector. Dr. Norman A. Doenges,

Professor of Classics, Dartmouth College, was field director. Dr. Antonio Arribas of the Universitat de les Illes Balears, Palma de Mallorca, was Director General of the Pollentia Excavations.[1]

3.2 Overview

Excavation in the Dartmouth College sector began with a limited objective. After removal of topsoil over the entire area of the forum in 1973 the top of an arch with a small hole beneath it appeared at the southwest corner of grid

[1] The author wishes to thank not only William J. Bryant but also Edward C. Lathem, Counselor to the President of Dartmouth College and Trustee of the Bryant Foundation, for the attentive and unwavering support he gave to the Department of Classics, the Archaeological Interns, the Field Director, and staff of the excavations. His thoughtful and gentle management contributed immeasurably to the efforts of all engaged in the excavations. Finally the author wishes to recognize members of the Classics Department, in particular Edward M. Bradley and Jeremy B. Rutter, for their help in selecting the Bryant Archaeological Interns and for their encouragement over the years.

Fig. 3.2 View of the Dartmouth Sector from the northeast. In the foreground are Rooms Q, U1, and U2. Beyond are Rooms V, X, and Y.

Square I-19. It was not clear at the time whether the arch was built over a cistern or a well. The Dartmouth College team set out to investigate the arch and to explore any structures related to it. Excavation revealed that the arch belonged to a well situated at the center of an independent complex of rooms west of the shops along the west side of the forum of Pollentia. (Fig. 3.1) The complex is made up of eight rooms only one of which (Room T) may be connected to the forum shops. Three of the rooms (V, X, and Y) on the west side of the complex are at a lower depth and constitute a separate unit without connection to the five rooms to the east. These western rooms face a street running north to south parallel to the west side of the forum. The five rooms to the east (U1, U2, Q, T, and R) are at a higher level, that of the floor of the forum. Their entrance faces north. It is probable that there was a second street running west to east along the north side of the complex, but that street has not yet been investigated. The area excavated from 1986 to 1993 measures 20.00 m. east to west x 13.70 m. north to south, an area of 274 sq. m. (Fig. 3.2)

3.3 The Western Unit: Rooms V, X, and Y

Rooms V, X, and Y constitute a separate unit at a lower depth having no apparent connection with the five rooms to the east. This western unit measures 10.22 m. east to west x 11.25 m. south to north. It is separated from the eastern unit by walls 20108 and 106. The unit faces west. The principal entrances to the unit are by way of expansive doorways from the western street into Rooms

V and Y. There may have been a secondary entrance into Room V from a north street, but a trench of the earlier excavators has removed the north wall of Room V and any evidence of a street or path along the north side of the complex.

3.3.1 The West Street

The west street runs north to south along the entire west side of the complex. Only a section of the street, 12.20 m. north to south x 3.40 m. east to west, was excavated by 1995. The surface of the street is very compact beaten earth gray in color. The street pavement west of Room V is at a consistent depth of 2.58-2.65 from south to north.[2] Immediately outside the entrances to Rooms V and Y the surface is somewhat lower perhaps as a result of traffic from the rooms onto the street.

Over the pavement of the street there was typical destruction fill, reddish earth mixed with clay and mud brick. But along the line of the threshold to Room Y there was a layer of crumbly burnt mud brick, 0.05 to 0.08 m. deep, directly over the pavement, and above the burnt mud brick was debris, mainly roof tiles, all apparently from the fire which destroyed Room Y. At the southwest corner of Room V the fill over the

---

[2] All depth figures are readings down from the bench mark set for the Ca'n Reinés site. Thus the larger the figure the lower the depth or level. The bench mark is 12.00 m. above sea level.

pavement was powdery gray earth with some signs of burning in it but without a distinct burnt layer directly over the surface of the street. There was, however, considerable destruction debris with signs of burning over the street in front of the entrance to Room V. But the quantity of archaeological material in the fill decreased noticeably with distance from the structure. Scattered throughout the reddish earth and clay destruction fill well above the pavement were roof tile fragments and some pottery, mainly amphora fragments.

Lying on or just above the surface of the street west of Room V were three bronze coins, all too worn to attribute. Between the west end of Wall 107 and the built corner there was a sestertius of Alexander Severus (222-235 A.D.) in destruction fill 0.08 m. above the pavement. Other objects of interest found in the destruction fill on or just above the street include:

A bone pin or needle, 0.10 m. long.

A conical bone ring, 0.043 m. in diameter x 0.028 tall, with two incised parallel lines at the top and bottom and four holes perhaps for receiving a bone or wire pin. The ring may have been used to hold hair in place.

Fragment of a roof tile with the stamp L Herenn[ius].

Roof tile fragment with the stamp HROT.

Two broken lead rings, one 0.075 m. in diameter and the other 0.09 in diameter.

Two bronze rings, one 0.085 m. in diameter and the other 0.023 in diameter.

A thin bronze finger ring, 0.018 m. in diameter.

A bronze eyelet with a short iron bar, 0.04 m. long, through the eye.

A bronze tool, 0.12 m. long, with a handle section, 0.03 m. long, for holding a wooden handle. Possibly a file.

Iron *falx* or sickle, 0.12 x 0.05 m.

At a distance 1.40 m. west of Wall 101 over the street is a massive built corner, solidly constructed out of marés blocks. (Fig. 3.3) The wall running north from the corner is made up of three rows of blocks set one above the other in two columns. The wall projecting eastward from the corner is directly in line with Wall 107. As a result, it was at first thought that the built corner represented the southwest corner of Room V. But after excavation it is clear that the built corner is not related to the third century A.D. structures. It rests on destruction fill 0.30 m. above the surface of the street. The top of the corner is at depth 1.73, significantly higher than other walls on the site. The corner, therefore, belongs to a structure built after the collapse of Room V. No other remains of the structure have been identified on the site.

Southeast from the built corner still over the street in Square H-22 is a rectangular section of *opus signinum* pavement, 1.40 x 1.30 x 0.10 m. thick, oriented due west to east. The pavement at depth 1.82 rests on a deep layer of destruction debris. There was evidence in section along the west side of square H-21 that a mud brick wall, 0.65 m. wide, projected east from the southeast corner of the pavement over Room Y. A single marés block was still in place on top of the mud brick wall on its north side. This mud brick wall rested on destruction debris over the floor of Room Y. The cement pavement and the mud brick wall are oriented neither with the built corner nor with the third century A.D. structures. It is, therefore, probable that they like the built corner are late-Roman or post-Roman in date. It is, however, the case that fragments of pinkish *opus signinum* pavement can be seen built into several walls of third century date west of the forum. A section of such pavement was found apparently purposely placed at floor level along the north side of Block 100 in Room V. Several large fragments of the pavement were found in destruction fill at the center of Room V west of the block and in destruction fill east of the entrance to Room V. The fragments found in Room V and perhaps the large section over the West Street may have come from an upper floor or loft in Room V. A similar rectangular section of *opus signinum* pavement can be seen at roughly the same depth on the surface of the field east of Room Q in Square J-18 which has not yet been excavated.

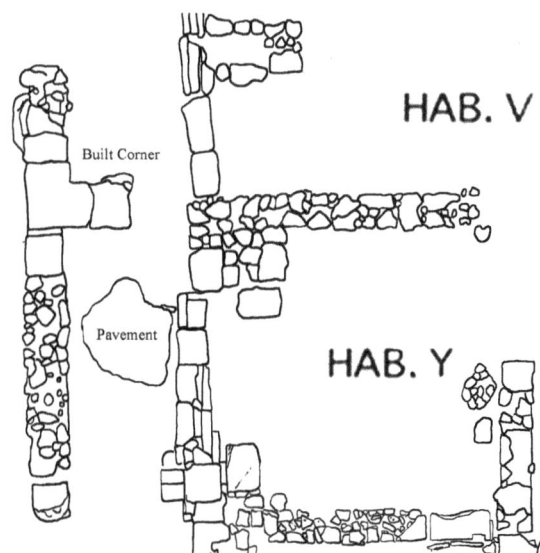

Fig. 3.3 Late built corner and opus signinum pavement over the West Street

The West Street running northwest to southeast along the west side of the complex of shops at the northwest corner of the forum is the first street west of the open area of the forum. It can be seen by extension as running along the east side of the Sa Portella excavation site. The structural complex on the west side of the forum is five rooms (26.00 m.) deep including the shops opening onto the forum. Evidence from the Dartmouth sector and the Sa Portella site indicates that Pollentia was planned with standard insulae, 26.00 m. (=87 Roman feet) wide east to west. The identification of the west street is an important factor in understanding the overall city plan of Pollentia.

3.3.2 Room Y

Room Y is located at the southwest corner of the west unit. It measures 4.30 m. east to west x 4.50 m. south to north. It is bound on the north by Wall 107, on the east by Wall 102, on the south by Wall 101, and on the west by the large Threshold 108.

Wall 107 along the north side of Room Y is the main wall running east and west from the well through the center of the complex. In Room Y this wall was broken 3.90 m. east from its west end by the digging of Snail Shell Pit A. The wall stands 0.96 m. high from the latest floor of the room. It is constructed from large and small marés blocks in irregular ashlar courses bonded with mud or clay. Wall 107 separates Room Y from Room V to the north.

Wall 102, the east wall of Room Y, runs north from the west end of Wall 101 in Room X. It is properly the west wall of Room X. The wall stands 0.80 m. high above the latest floor and is made up of nine regular courses of small marés blocks bonded with mud or clay. The wall is finished at the top with four large blocks which may have served as a sill for the mud brick section above. Near its south end a patch of stucco still clings to the west face of the wall. At the north end of the wall is a large door jamb block, 0.64 m. tall. This block indicates that there was a doorway between Room Y and Room X at the northeast corner of the room. The doorway was destroyed by the digging of Snail Shell pit A. Blocks from the north end of Wall 102 were found at the bottom of the pit.

The south wall of Room Y was almost completely robbed after the collapse of the room. Only a few stones from the lowest course of the wall have survived, but they include a large block at its west end which may have served as the cornerstone for the general complex. A line of brown compact earth with marés chips in it quite distinct from the pavement of the room marks the position of the wall. There was no burnt layer, rubble, or other sign of fire over the brown compact earth, an indication that the wall was removed after the destruction of the room. In a sounding excavated at the southwest corner of the room in 1995 a section of the wall two courses high was exposed. The upper course is a flat stone, 0.23 long x 0.07 m. tall. Beneath it is a larger ashlar block, 0.43 long x 0.10 m. tall. The bottom of this block is at depth 2.86. Beneath the larger block is a thick round footing stone, 0.24 wide x 0.15 m. tall. The footing stone rests on earth at depth 3.01. Thus the wall was built on the earliest Roman pavement in the room and may, therefore, be dated to the mid-first century B.C. It is the continuation into Room Y of the earlier wall identified in 1997 below Wall 101 in Room X. This earlier wall ran under later Wall 101 at least to the line of

Wall 106, the east wall of Room X. Room Y, therefore, was originally a single large room corresponding to Room V to the north. It was divided in two by the construction of Room X in the late first century B.C. or early first century A.D.

At the southeast corner of the room where Wall 101 meets Wall 102 there is a doorway, 0.90 m. wide, marked by two steps from Room Y to a higher level. The lower step at depth 2.41 is a large block much worn along its north side. The second step is of beaten earth at depth 2.33. Its riser from the lower step is made up of two thin stones set vertically along the north side of the step. North of the lower step a half column drum was placed on the floor of Room Y as an additional step and north of the column drum there was a rectangular marés block set perhaps to provide additional access to the steps. These steps lead to an alley or walkway, 1.10 m. wide, of compact brown earth at depths 2.33 to 2.41 between Room Y and Room Z to the south. The surface of the walkway is very firm almost like marés. Along the south side of the walkway against the north wall of Room Z runs a border of flat stones, 0.40 m. wide. There was no evidence of fire over the upper step and the walkway, suggesting that the walkway was not in use when Rooms Y and Z were destroyed. At some point before the collapse of the rooms the walkway was blocked by a wall at its west end. A round hole through this wall suggests that in its second stage the passageway served as a drainage ditch between the two rooms. Powdery gray earth with much pottery in it accumulated over the walkway to depth 2.23-2.25. On the surface of this powdery gray fill was a short (1.50 m. long) shallow channel of burnt mud brick in which a wooden beam may have burned. There were also several large building blocks lying flat on the surface or embedded deep in the powdery fill. Above this soft surface was reddish gray destruction fill with many small stones and roof tiles in it. The presence of the loose blocks in front of the lower step suggests that the stairs leading to the walkway were still in use when Room Y burned. But in the powdery fill over the walkway and the line of Wall 101 at its west end there were fragments of hand-made Talayotic and Campanian B wares along with 22 fragments of Arretine and Gallic Sigillata wares and quantities of Roman common pottery but only 32 fragments of *terra sigillata Africana* A and one fragment of *terra sigillata Africana* C. On the evidence of the pottery the fill and thus the closing of the walkway date to the late first or early second century A.D.[3]

The main feature of the west wall of Room Y is a large threshold, 2.60 north to south x 0.40-0.48 m. east to west at depth 2.56-2.59. South of the threshold between it and the cornerstone of Wall 101 are two large building blocks which mark the south side of the entrance to the room. The threshold is made up of four large stones. The two southernmost stones are more worn from traffic on their

---

[3] For the use of the passageway as a drainage ditch and the built drain at a lower level see below p. 54.

east side than are the two northernmost blocks. The threshold thus marks a major exit from Room Y up to the level of the West Street. There was originally a channel, 0.13 m. wide, in the threshold similar to that in the entrance to Room V. The sides of this channel, however, were chiseled away at the south end of the doorway, and the threshold became only a broad, smooth step from Room Y up to the level of the street. At the south end of the threshold there is a cutting, 0.20 wide x 0.05 deep, through the entire width of the threshold into which the wooden frame for a door may have sat. Just north of this cutting on the surface of the threshold block there are two additional shallow cuttings, one 0.21 long, at the west edge of the threshold and a second slightly deeper one, 0.25 long, in the center channel. It is possible that these cuttings also held some kind of wood framing for a door. There are no cuttings of this sort at the north end of the threshold. There the west side of the channel remains partially preserved. The removal of the channel suggests that Room Y like Room V had originally a closed doorway and may have been used for industrial purposes, but it was then converted into a *taberna* or shop with open access from the street and with the entrance protected by a portico or a porch projecting into the street.

At the northwest corner of Room Y between the threshold and Wall 107 there is a built platform, 0.80 north to south x 1.46 east to west x 0.70 m. high. The platform is made up of the door jamb block at the north end of the threshold and a second large block to the east. Between the two blocks there may have been a shelf 0.20 m. deep. The platform stands against Wall 107 and seems to have resembled a modern barbecue pit. On the other hand, the platform may have been flat on top and may have served as a table or counter at the entrance to Room Y. At the southeast corner of the platform is a large block, 0.66 x 0.45 m., embedded in the floor of the room. The block may have served as a low step on which to stand at the platform.

At a distance 1.60 m. west from the threshold and the exit from Room Y there is a free-standing wall (22106) running south to north parallel to the threshold and set axially in front of the doorway. (Fig. 3.1) The wall is 4.18 m. long and stands 0.45 m. high. At its north end there is a large marés block 0.85 m. high. A leveling course indicates that a similar block stood at its south end. The block itself was found 1.00 m. west of the wall in destruction fill. This wall and blocks almost certainly belong to a roofed porch or portico projecting into the street in front of the entrance to Room Y. The porch would have protected the open entrance to the room from the elements. Upon leaving Room Y, a person would have met the low wall and then have to turn either north or south along the west street. A similar porch stood in front of Room Z in the third century A.D. There may have been initially a pilaster portico running along the front of all the shops on the West Street. In the third century low walls were added between the pilasters in front of Rooms Y and Z. See below pp. 52-54.

The latest floor of Room Y is of beaten earth at depth 2.63 near the southeast corner to 2.77 near the northwest corner. The pavement thus slopes gradually downward from southeast to northwest. Along the east wall of the room 1.20 m. from the southeast corner were two flat rectangular pieces of green marble which seemed to be in place on the floor. They may represent all that remains of a greenish marble border which ran around the sides of the room. Over the entire floor but especially toward the northwest corner of the room there was a layer of burnt debris, 0.30 to 0.50 m. deep, a mixture of broken roof tiles, amphora and pottery fragments, and burnt mud brick. The burnt rubble layer was especially deep in a circular area, 0.80 m. in diameter, southeast of the platform beneath the iron grate listed below. The burnt layer over the floor of the room ended along the line of the south wall. No evidence of burning was found south of the large stones at the south end of the threshold.

In the 1995 sounding at the southwest corner of the room there was evidence of three beaten earth pavements or floors in Room Y. The uppermost floor or surface on which the room collapsed is at depth 2.76 to 2.77. Pottery from the fill of the floor was two fragments of hand-made Talayotic ware, one fragment of Campanian black glaze ware, one fragment of fine-walled pottery, and two fragments of *terra sigillata Africana* A, suggesting a date for the pavement in the late first century A.D. Beneath this floor was a second floor at depth 2.85 to 2.87. On this floor a bronze coin too worn to attribute was found. Pottery in the fill of the floor was one fragment of hand-made Talayotic ware, four fragments of Campanian ware, two fragments of fine-walled pottery, and fourteen fragments of Roman common pottery. But included among the pottery were five fragments of *terra sigillata Africana* A and three fragments of North African common pottery, which would date the second pavement also to the late first century A.D.[4] The lowest pavement was at depth 3.20 to 3.21. Over this pavement was a thin burnt layer, and at the south side of the sounding there was a line of flat stones which may be the remains of a wall. Pottery beneath this pavement was eleven fragments of hand-made Talayotic ware, one fragment of an Ebusitan amphora, and one fragment of Roman common pottery. The pottery evidence suggests that this floor dates to the end of the Talayotic period. The earth above this floor in levels 5 and 4 of the sounding appears to have been a Roman fill to raise the general ground level of the area.

---

[4] Note that in two soundings excavated in Room X in 1993 (below, p. 31) and in a sounding at the southwest corner of Room V (below, p. 36) pottery found in the fill of this pavement dates the pavement unequivocally to the first century B.C. It is possible that the presence of African wares in levels 3 and 4 of the sounding is the result of filtration from above along the line of wall 101 when the wall was dismantled. The African ware fragments are all very small. The pavement and wall 101, thus, may properly date to the first century B.C. rather than the first century A.D.

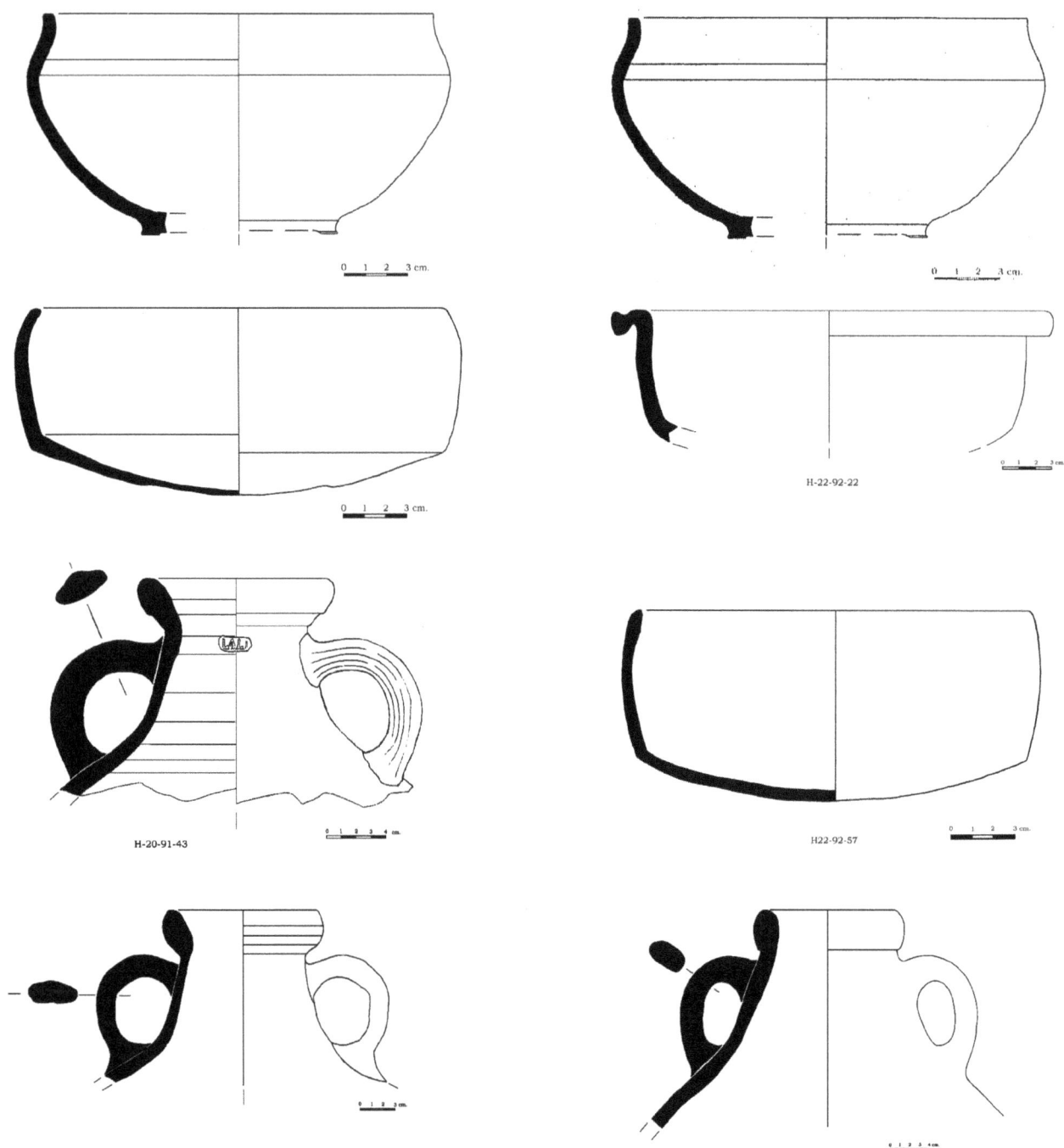

0   1   2   3 cm.

0   1   2   3 cm.

0   1   2   3 cm.

H-22-92-22

0   1   2   3 cm.

H-20-91-43

0   1   2   3   4 cm.

H22-92-57

0   1   2   3 cm.

0   1   2   3 cm.

0   1   2   3 cm.

Fig. 3.4 Sampling of pottery found in destruction fill throughout the sector

Above the burnt rubble layer on the latest floor of the room there was typical destruction fill, reddish earth mixed with mud brick and clay. Throughout this fill were many roof tile fragments. Datable pottery in the destruction fill and the burnt layer beneath it was north African *terra sigillata Africana* A and C north African common ware, and Roman common pottery dating to the second half of the third century A.D. (Fig. 3.4)

On or just above the floor of Room Y there were several objects of special interest:

Fragments from three broken amphoras along the south face of Wall 107.

A globular jug, 0.18 m. tall, complete except for a small section of its strap handle, found also along the south side of Wall 107 east of the platform.

28

Fig. 3.5 Iron window grate

An iron grate, 1.05 x 0.89 m., found 1.00 m. southeast from the platform on top of rubble 0.25 m. above floor level at depth 2.49 m. (Fig. 3.5) The grate has three horizontal bars intersected by five vertical bars. It does not have the usual stars at the intersection of the bars. The grate, therefore, may not have come from a window but may be related to the platform at the west end of Wall 107 on which it would fit.

A shallow bronze dish, 0.09 m. in diameter, with an omphalos in its center, found under the northwest corner of the grate.

An amphora, broken, found on the floor of the room near the north end of Wall 102.

A lead and iron tool, consisting of an iron bar with two lead side pieces. The tool resembles the handle of modern shovel.

An iron eyelet through which a rope or cord may have passed.

Two bronze fish hooks, contemporary in design, one found west of the north end of Wall 102 and the other in the center of the room.

A worked goat horn which may have been used as a scabbard for a short knife, found on the floor of the room under the iron grate.

An amphora, broken but restorable, in the circular depression east of the threshold.

Numerous fragments of at least two but possibly four amphoras found in burnt mud brick around the north and east sides of the large block south of the threshold. The amphoras once stood on the floor of the room just inside the south end of the entrance.

Fragments of nineteen identifiable amphoras which stood mainly along the north wall of the room, around the counter at the northwest corner, and at the south end of the doorway to the room. Almost all of the amphoras are of types Africana I and II dating to the third century A. D.

Five bronze plates found just south of the platform and east of the threshold.

Five small rectangular and triangular iron plates with projecting nails or spikes, found east of the threshold.

A round ceramic disk, 0.04 m. in diameter, and a round ceramic base, 0.065 m. in diameter, found east from the threshold.

These articles, especially the amphoras found along the north wall of the room and south of the doorway as well as the platform and the fish hooks suggest that Room Y was a shop or *taberna* in which food was served. It had a broad doorway to the street with a covered porch in front of the doorway. The deep layer of burnt debris over the latest floor of the room indicates that Room Y was destroyed by an intense fire which seems to have started near the northwest corner of the room.

At some point after the destruction of Room Y an oval refuse pit (Snail Shell Pit A), 1.90 east to west x ca. 2.00 m. south to north was dug through the mound of earth over the room at its northeast corner directly north of Wall 102. (Fig. 3.6) The digging of this pit destroyed the north end of Wall 102 where it may have joined Wall 107. The pit also cut through and destroyed Wall 107 4.20 m. from its west end. The bottom of the pit broke through the pavement of Rooms Y, X, and V in the area north of Wall 102. The outline of Snail Shell Pit A was clearly visible in section along the south side of Square I-21. Many stones from the destroyed walls were found at the bottom of the pit. The fill in the pit was clayey earth mixed with mud brick somewhat looser and lighter in color than typical destruction fill. Throughout the pit there were many snail shells, but at its bottom was a deep pile of shells which had been thrown into the pit. Pottery in the pit was mainly north African and Roman common pottery, but there were also several sherds of Islamic painted ware. At the bottom of the pit where it broke through the floor of the room several sherds of Campanian A pottery, Iberian pottery, and hand-made Talayotic wares were recovered. The Islamic pottery suggests that all three snail shell pits on the site date to the period of Islamic occupation on Mallorca.

3.3.3 Room X

Room X lies east of Room Y. It is roughly square in shape, measuring 4.40 m. east to west x 4.40 m. south to north. It is bound on the north by Wall 107, on the east by Wall 106, on the south by Wall 101, and on the west by Wall 102. Wall 107, the north wall of the room, is broken 1.70 m. west from the northeast corner of the room. Many stones from the break spilled into Room X to the south and into Room V to the north. At a distance of 3.10 from the northeast corner of the room two blocks from the lowest course of the wall may still be in place. This break in the wall resulted from the digging of Snail Shell Pit C. (Fig. 3.6) Along the line of Wall 107 in the

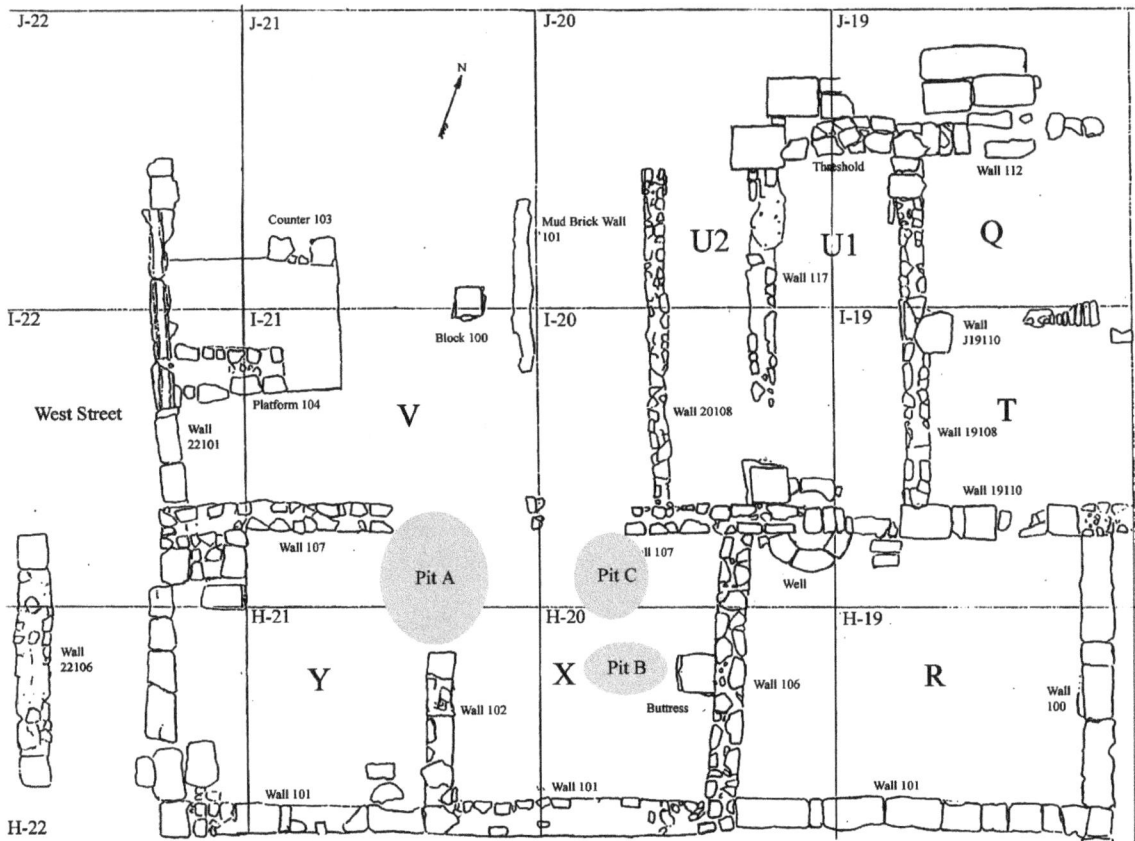

Fig. 3.6 Snail Shell Pits in Rooms Y and X

break there was a mass of snail shells at the bottom of the pit. The wall stands 1.00 m. high above the latest floor of Room X near the northeast corner of the room. It is solidly built with three regular courses of large blocks at the bottom and four courses of smaller blocks at the top, all bonded with mud or clay.

Wall 106 butts up against Wall 107. It is not bonded to Wall 107, nor is it absolutely perpendicular to that wall. Its most prominent feature is four large reused blocks standing upright on their short sides and built into the wall. Smaller blocks and roof tiles in irregular courses were laid around the four large blocks. These large blocks may have made the wall somewhat unstable. To strengthen the wall, a buttress was built at the center of the wall 1.80 m. north from the southeast corner of the room. The buttress is 1.17 m. tall and is made up of rectangular blocks measuring 0.60 x 0.55 m. The wall at the buttress stands 1.36 m. high above the latest floor of the room. Both the construction of wall 106 out of reused blocks and the fact that it rests on the latest floor of the room at depth 2.60 indicate that the wall is late. The northernmost large block, almost certainly taken from another structure, rests on a packing of earth at depth 2.47. A small section of an earlier phase of the wall remains in place at the southwest corner of Room R. The south wall of the room, Wall 101, is poorly preserved at its center. It joins Wall 106 to which it is bonded at the southeast corner of the room and Wall 102 at the southwest corner. It is constructed out of four

irregular courses of larger blocks at the bottom of the wall with smaller blocks or stones above. The wall has sagged noticeably at the southeast corner of the room. There it stands 1.37 m. high above the latest floor of the room. At the southwest corner of the room it is only 0.90 m. high. The courses are bonded with mud or clay. The entire north face of the wall was covered with a thick coating of soft white clay. Whether this clay served as a kind of plaster on the wall is unclear. It may have come from imperfectly hardened mud bricks above the stone sill.

A sounding excavated in the summer of 1997 against the north face of the wall revealed the existence of an earlier wall beneath Wall 101. Two courses of this lower wall were visible from depth 2.51 to 2.79. Beneath these two courses are footing stones to depth 3.08. The wall, it appears, was constructed on a surface (Level 5 in the sounding) dating on the basis of the pottery in the fill to the second half of the first century B.C. The later or upper wall dating to the third century A.D. rests directly on the lower wall which is the continuation eastward of the wall identified in the sounding excavated at the southwest corner of Room Y in 1995.[5] It is also possible that the lower wall should be regarded as three courses high from depth 2.51 to 2.93-2.94. If so, it was constructed on a surface (level 7 in the sounding) which

---

[5] See above p. 27.

may be dated on the basis of the pottery in that stratum to the first half of the first century B.C.

The west wall of Room X, Wall 102, ends in a large door jamb block, 2.50 from the southwest corner of the room. North of the door jamb block there was a doorway into the room from Room Y. The north end of Wall 102 was destroyed by the digging of Snail Shell Pit A. No threshold stone at the doorway has been preserved. There may also have been a doorway from Room X into Room V through Wall 107 at the northwest corner of the room. Such a doorway, if it existed, would also have been destroyed by Snail Shell Pit A. Wall 102 is made up of six regular courses of marés blocks bonded with mud or clay. At its south end it stands 0.90 m. high above the latest floor of the room, at its north end 0.53 m. high. The top course of larger stones preserved on the west side of the wall is missing on the east side.

Wall 102 like Wall 106 is bonded to upper Wall 101, the south wall of the room. This wall in all probability was also built up against Wall 107 at its north end. Room X, therefore, constitutes a unit constructed south of Wall 107. As the three walls fit together, it is likely that they were built at the same time. In its earliest phase Room X may have been constructed no earlier than the end of the first century B.C. or the beginning of the first century A.D. when the ground level was raised to depth 2.60. The evidence from Wall 106, however, suggests that the existing walls date to the third century. They may have replaced earlier walls. Room Y, on the other hand, at a lower depth than Room X, was part of the original construction dating to the mid-first century B.C. It may initially have been a single large room like Room V extending eastward to the line of Wall 106.

In the summer of 1993 two stratigraphic soundings were made in Room X, one at the juncture of walls 107 and 106 in the northeast corner of the room and the other near the northwest corner of the room. In the first sounding six strata were identified. Stratum 1, the latest floor of the room over which was the burnt layer of the destruction fill, is reddish crumbly earth at depths 2.57 to 2.64. Stratum 2 is beaten earth with small stones packed into it to form a solid pavement with loose gray earth beneath from depths 2.64 to 2.70. Stratum 3, the level of the floor of Room V, is yellow earth with plaster in it at depths 2.70 to 2.79. Stratum 4 is yellow earth without plaster at depths 2.79 to 2.84. Stratum 5 is compact crumbly greenish earth with stones at depths 2.84 to 2.94. Finally stratum 6 is brownish red compact earth which breaks into clumps from depths 2.94 to 3.19. At depth 3.11 in stratum 6 there is a large ashlar block which appears to be the footing for Wall 107. Pottery in stratum 1 was Roman Republican amphora fragments. In strata 2 to 5 the pottery was seven fragments of hand-made Talayotic ware together with one fragment of Campanian A, five fragments of fine wall ware, four fragments of locally made Roman Republican common pottery, and one Roman amphora fragment. In stratum 6 to bedrock there were three hand-made Talayotic

fragments, two fragments of fine wall wares, and three Roman amphora fragments.

The second sounding was made at the east side of Snail Shell Pit A, taking advantage of the fact that the pit had broken through the latest floor of the room. In the sounding eight strata were identified. Stratum 1 is brownish crumbly earth, the latest floor of the room, from depths 2.60 to 2.67. Stratum 2 is gray loose earth from depths 2.67 to 2.71. Stratum 3 is reddish earth with clay from depths 2.71 to 2.78. Stratum 4 is again brown compact earth from depths 2.78 to 2.87. Stratum 5 represents a marked change to yellow earth with bits of carbon in it at depths 2.87 to 2.99. Stratum 6 is a thin layer of clay at depths 2.99 to 3.02. Stratum 7 is gray loose earth at depths 3.02 to 3.12. Stratum 8 is compact reddish or brown earth which breaks into clumps at depths 3.12 to 3.33. Beneath this level there is very dark gray to black compact earth with no archaeological materials. In strata 1-4 there was a moderate amount of pottery, mainly north African wares, but also Talayotic, Iberian, and Punic amphora fragments. In strata 5-8 there was considerably less pottery. Pottery in stratum 8 was two fragments of hand-made Talayotic ware, two fragments of Iberian pottery, and fragments of Ebusitan amphoras.

Fig. 3.7 Cylindrical bone hinge

The latest floor of Room X is of beaten earth. It slopes gradually downward from north to south from depth 2.58 at Wall 107 to 2.63 at Wall 101. The evidence from the stratigraphical soundings indicates that there were two earlier floors in the room, one of beaten earth with pebbles set into it at depth 2.64-2.67 and a still earlier beaten earth floor at depth 2.70-277. On the floor at depth 2.64-2.67 there was a cylindrical bone hinge with incised parallel lines at one end and drilled attachment holes. (Fig. 3.7) As the pottery beneath the two lower floors was mainly hand-made Talayotic ware with a fragment of Campanian ware, fine wall wares, and locally made Roman Republican common pottery, the two earlier floors seem to date to the first century B.C., the third or latest floor to the end of the first century B.C.

or the beginning of the first century A.D.[6] As the two early floors were laid in association with the earliest walls of the complex, notably Wall 107 and lower Wall 101 , they date the construction of Rooms V and Y to the first half of the first century B.C. Room X seems to have been added later perhaps early in the first century A.D. But note that the existing walls of the room may date to the mid-third century A.D.

The data with respect to earlier floors beneath the destruction surface in Room X were confirmed in the sounding excavated in the summer of 1997 at the south side of the room against Wall 101. In that sounding four floors or surfaces were identified. The uppermost on which the room collapsed is at depth 2.57 and may be dated on the basis of the pottery in the fill of the surface to the end of the first century B.C. or the beginning of the first century A.D. Beneath it was a surface at depth 2.63-2.64 (level 2 in the sounding). Pottery in the fill dates this surface toward the end of the first century B.C. somewhat earlier than the date of the destruction surface. A third surface was at depth 2.77-2.79 (level 5 in the sounding). Pottery in the fill suggests a date early in the second half of the first century B.C. for the floor. Finally there was a surface at depth 2.90 (level 7 in the sounding). Pottery in the fill suggests a date in the first half of the first century B.C. for this surface.

West of the buttress block on Wall 106 Snail Shell Pit B broke through the latest floor of the room to depth 2.70. (Fig. 3.6) Snail shell Pit B was oval in shape, measuring approximately 1.20 m. north to south x 1.30 m. west to east. Fill in the pit was reddish earth mixed with clay. Pottery recovered from the pit included Roman common wares, north African *terra sigillata Africana* A and C, and two sherds of Islamic ware. Like Pit A this pit seems to date to the period of Islamic occupation of Mallorca.

Destruction fill in Room X over the latest floor was reddish earth mixed with mud brick and clay. Along the line of Wall 106 the fill was dark red compact mud brick which had fallen perhaps from the wall. Directly over the floor of the room was a shallow burnt layer, noticeable especially on the west side of the room. Above the burnt layer there was destruction debris, mainly roof tile fragments, 0.30 m. deep. An intense fire seems to have destroyed the room.
Room X was unusually rich in objects of interest. Of greatest importance are twenty four amphoras found lying on the floor around the west and south sides of the room. An additional amphora was found standing upright at the northwest corner of the buttress. Almost all of the amphoras are north African (form Dressel 30), dating to the second half of the third century. (Fig. 3.8) Two of the amphoras may be Ebusitan in origin. An

amphora at the north end of wall 102 contained fine white sand. Another at the southeast corner of the room held a mass of minuscule fish bones, perhaps the residue of the fish sauces *garum* or *salsamentum*. The inside of an amphora lying along Wall 101 was coated with pitch. It as well as one in the center of the room contained organic material which remains unidentified.

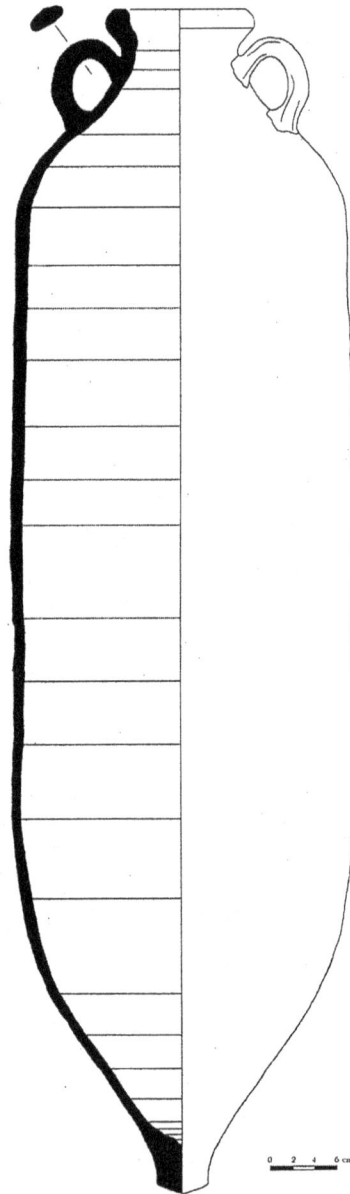

H-21-91-18

Fig. 3.8 One of the amphorae found on the floor of Room X

Leaning upright against the north face of Wall 101, 1.50 m. from the southeast corner of the room were four unbroken roof tiles. The inner three tiles were almost completely encased in the heavy coating of clay on the face of the wall. A fifth roof tile, cracked but complete, was leaning against the clay coating west of the other four. The fifth tile was stamped with the almost illegible letters CNIFI in an incuse square. Finally standing up

---

[6] In the fill of the latest pavement there was an absence of Talayotic pottery fragments. Found were three Roman amphora fragments, one Ebusitan amphora fragment, and six fragments of north African common ware. The area excavated was very limited.

against the northernmost roof tile was a large ceramic basin, 0.70 in diameter x 0.20 m. deep. The basin has a flaring lip with a pouring spout on one side. The roof tiles and the basin were purposely placed in the position in which they were found against the wall.

Lying on the floor along the west side of Room X parallel to Wall 102 at its north end and 0.10 m. from the wall was a heavy iron ingot, 1.00 long x 0.10 m. in diameter. A second iron ingot, also 1.00 long x 0.10 m. in diameter, was lying at a 30° angle to Wall 101 just west of the roof tiles. The fifth roof tile was propped against the wall over the east end of this ingot. The ingots are solid iron cast perhaps to a standard length, diameter, and weight.

Projecting downward to the southeast from Wall 102 over the end of the first iron ingot 1.35 m. north from the southwest corner of Room X was a cover tile (imbrex) 0.50 m. long. The tile looked much like a drain coming from the wall into the room. A similar cover tile, 0.40 m. long projected into the room from the east Wall 106, 1.00 m. north from the southeast corner of the room. Because there are no holes through the walls above the tiles, it is not clear what function these projecting tiles served. They seemed, however, to have been placed purposely in the positions in which they were found.

Along the north side of the room south of Wall 107 were several objects of interest lying on the latest floor of the room. From east to west they include:

A small jug or pitcher, unbroken, found 0.50 m. west from Wall 106

The neck and shoulder of an amphora. Fragments from this amphora were scattered throughout the destruction fill at the northeast corner of the room.

An iron ring, 0.17 in diameter x 0.055 m. wide, found lying over the balance arm.

A bronze balance arm, 0.33 m. long, found 1.04 m. west from Wall 106.

A set of three iron rings nested together. The outer ring is 0.20 in diameter x 0.08 m. wide, the second ring 0.17 m. in diameter, and the third ring 0.12 m. in diameter.

A tubular iron stand with two tubular legs, 0.13 m. long, ending in iron wheels or knobs. Over one leg was a bronze disk. Two bronze nails going perhaps with the disk lay nearby. The function of this object is uncertain. A ceramic bowl, 0.24 m. in diameter, lying just north of the nested rings. The bowl was discolored gray to black by fire.

A bronze funnel, 0.26 m. tall, flattened on the floor of the room.

An iron fire tong with a hook at one end, 0.50 m. long.

A second iron tong without a hook, 0.40 m. long.

An iron roller (?) with an arch handle, 0.14 x 0.13 m. Four well preserved bronze nails were found around this object. The function of the object is uncertain, but it looks like a modern cookie or pasta roller.

A third iron ring broken, 0.13 in diameter x 0.055 m. wide.

Immediately south of the break in Wall 107 were the following objects on the latest floor of the room:

Handle of a bronze jug with a woman's head and oriental symbols in relief, 0.18 m. long. (Fig. 3.9)

Fig. 3.9 Handle from a bronze jug

Bronze nail or furniture fitting, 0.12 m. long

Handle from a lead jug or pitcher, 0.13 m. long

Another iron ring, 0.12 m. in diameter x 0.05 wide.

A small iron ring, 0.06 m. in diameter.

An iron knife blade, 0.18 m. long.

A bronze knife handle ending in a ram's head, 0.14 m. long. The knife handle and blade were found together at the base of Wall 107 on the floor of the room.

Elsewhere in the room the following objects were found:

A half coin, not attributable, found on the floor of the room under an amphora.

A bronze frying pan, 0.15 in diameter x 0.06 deep x 0.31 m. long. The handle of the pan is scalloped. The pan was found at the southeast corner of the room (Fig. 3.10)

Fig. 3.10 Small frying pan found at the southeast corner of Room X.

A second bronze frying pan, 0.15 m. in diameter, with a perforated handle, 0.12 m. long. It lay at the south face of the buttress to Wall 106.

Two thin bronze plates, one rectangular with three bronze nails still in place and one circular in shape with part of a bronze key attached.

An iron wire bucket handle, 0.12 m. long.

A bent iron strip with an iron nail in it, 0.16 long x 0.035 m. wide.

An iron handle, 0.20 long x 0.02 m. wide.

The range and variety of these objects found in Room X suggest that the room was used for storage perhaps in relation to Room Y which fronted on the street. The amphoras seem to have been placed along the west and south walls of the room. The basin and roof tiles were stacked against the south wall. At the northeast corner of the room there may have been a small work area. The center of the room was largely open and uncluttered.

3.3.4 Room V

Room V is located north of Rooms Y and X. It is the largest room in the complex, measuring 8.10 west to east x 5.85 m. south to north. It is bound on the west by Wall 101, on the east by Wall 108, and on the south by Wall

107. The north wall of the room was destroyed by a trench of the earlier excavators, but its position may be surmised from the location of the large threshold in Square J-20. The north end of Wall 108 was also cut off by the trench of the earlier excavators.

Wall 101 is 5.85 m. long. At its south end it butts up against Wall 107. At that end it is two courses high. The lower course is a single heavy ashlar block, 0.65 long x 0.30 m. high. Above it is a smaller block, 0.60 long x 0.09 m. high. The wall was constructed on the earliest pavement in Room V at depth 2.86. Beneath the wall proper are four levels of large footing stones to depth 3.37. They provide a solid base for the wall. The main feature of the wall is a wide entrance to Room V from the west street. The doorway measures 3.60 m. and is centered on the west side of the room. The threshold is made up of three marés blocks which turned red in color as a result of the intense fire to which they were subjected when the room was destroyed. Because of the softness of the stones they are heavily damaged on both the street and the room side also perhaps as a consequence of the fire. The two northernmost blocks are narrow, 0.30 to 0.40 m. wide, and are irregular in shape because of erosion. The most northerly block is 1.30 m. long, the middle block 1.40 m. long. The southernmost block is 0.90 m. long. On its east side it was cut back to accommodate platform 104. Through the middle of all the blocks runs a channel, 0.14 wide x 0.03 m. deep, for holding the wood entrance closure. At the north end of the doorway the walls of the channel are worn away perhaps by the feet of those entering Room V through a door in the closure. Near the north end there are two iron pins or bolts set into the center of the channel of the doorway. The first pin is 0.17 south from the north end of the entrance. The second pin is 0.48 south of the first or 0.65 from the north end of the entrance. These pins suggest that the channel may have held a wooden plate or sill where a door once stood.

North of the doorway Wall 101 is preserved for a distance of only 1.00 m. At its north end there was a thick layer of clay or plaster which has fallen to the north in an arc from the wall. On its west or street side this section of the wall is three ashlar courses high and seems to rest on the pavement of the west street. On its east side only the uppermost course and the bottommost course of the wall are preserved. Only a single block of the lowest course, perhaps the footing for the wall, has survived. The top of this block is at depth 2.77, the level of the floor of Room V. The block rests on fill at depth 3.03. Beneath the block was a shallow empty hole. There is no sign of a wall running east from Wall 101 as the northwest corner of Room V was destroyed by the trench of the earlier excavators.

The east Wall 108 of Room V is 5.60 m. long. At its south end it butts up against Wall 107 and is not bonded to that wall. Its north end was destroyed by the trench of the earlier excavators. At its present north end Wall 108 is nine ashlar courses high. A sounding at the north end revealed that beneath the ashlar courses on the west side of the wall in Room V there is a wide footing stone at depth 2.78. This footing block rests on a packing of field stones to depth 3.04. It seems clear that Wall 108 like other walls of the complex was constructed by placing leveling stones in a deep trench. Over the leveling stones a wide footing was set to support the ashlar courses of the wall above. The footing stone at depth 2.78 was designed to accommodate a pavement in Room V at depths 2.73 to 2.75. At its south end where it meets Wall 107 the wall is 0.97 m. high. The whole of its west face is plastered except for a vertical gap 0.55 m. wide, 2.85 m. north from wall 107. It is possible that a mud brick wall ran west from this gap in the plaster, but there was no evidence during excavation for the existence of such a wall on the floor of the room. The outline of whole mud bricks, however, which fell in no clear pattern did appear in section west of Block 100 in the center of the room, suggesting the possibility of a wall. Set into the pavement at the base of Wall 108, 2.10 m. north from the southeast corner of the room, is a rectangular block 0.60 x 0.40 m. In this block there are two shallow square cuttings, 0.13 x 0.13 m., 0.20 m. apart. The function of this block is unclear. But the two square cuttings suggest that the block served as a base for wooden posts supporting a beam or beams carrying an upper floor or loft at the east side of the room. Wall 108 is constructed with marés blocks bonded with clay in regular courses. There are larger blocks in the four lower courses with courses of smaller blocks above. In spite of its solid foundation the top of the wall bulges slightly eastward at its center.

The south wall of the room, Wall 107, was broken 0.50 m. west from the southeast corner of the room by the digging of Snail Shell Pit C. It was broken as well 3.50 m. east from the southwest corner of the room by the digging of Snail Shell Pit A. Between the two pits two blocks from the bottom of the wall and three blocks possibly from the top of the wall remained in place. Snail shell pit C was oval in shape, 2.00 north to south x 1.20 m. east to west. (Fig. 3.5) Many stones from Wall 107 remained in the pit along its east side. In the powdery gray fill of the pit there were several sherds of Islamic pottery. At the bottom of the pit where it broke through the floor of Room V there were sherds of hand-made Talayotic wares, Iberian painted wares, and Campanian A pottery. Wall 107 at its west end is made up of five regular courses of large marés blocks bonded with mud or clay. It stands 0.88 m. high above the latest floor of the room. The regular courses of the wall, however, end abruptly 1.40 m. east from the southwest corner of the room. West of the line of the regular courses there is an addition to the wall out of more irregular blocks of varying size. On the south side of this addition is the platform at the northwest corner of Room Y. In a 1995 sounding at the southwest corner of the room it was learned that the west end of Wall 107 facing room V is only three courses high. The lowest course is a solid ashlar block, 0.70 long x 0.30 m. tall. The second course is another large block, 0.50 long x 0.15 m. tall.

The third course is a smaller block, 0.10 m. tall. Above the third course the north face of the wall has been robbed. The bottom of Wall 107 is at depth 3.10. There are no leveling stones supporting the wall.

At a distance 2.00 m. west from Wall 108 is mud brick Wall 101, 3.00 m. long, running north to south parallel to Wall 108 and standing 0.50 m. east of block 100. Its north end was cut by the trench of the earlier excavators. It ends abruptly 1.00 m. south of Block 100. The wall is 0.30 m. wide, the length of a single mud brick. It was plastered on both sides. During excavation two lines of the plaster could be seen clearly in the concentrated dark red mud brick fill east of the block. These lines indicated that the wall fell eastward when the room collapsed. The outline of mud bricks from the wall was clearly visible in section along the west side of Square I-20. Unfortunately a clandestine excavator dug through the wall and destroyed much of it during the winter of 1991. It was possible to preserve only the lowest 0.20 m. of the wall. The wall was constructed on the floor of Room V. Its function is not certain, but it may have served to delimit a storage area along the east side of Room V. An iron wheel, an iron saw, two bronze frying pans, and two lamps were found east of the wall. The coins found along the line of the wall may have been hidden in it or were in a bag on shelves along the wall.

At a distance 2.80 m. west from Wall 108 and 3.00 m. north of Wall 107 is a free-standing Block 100, 0.50 x 0.48 x 0.82 m. tall. The block is made up of two large reused marés building stones. The lower stone is slightly larger than the upper one and has a deep vertical cutting on its east side near the northeast corner. The function of this block is not clear. But it may have served as a base for a mud brick column supporting a loft at the east side of the room. The outline of several mud bricks could be seen in section west of the block during excavation. Several large pieces of pink *opus signinum* pavement, one 1.50 x 0.50 x 0.20 m. in size, perhaps from the loft floor were found in destruction fill in the area of the block.[7] Block 100 as it now stands was part of a late remodeling of the room.

Projecting 1.30 m. eastward into Room V from Wall 101 at the south end of the entrance to the room is Platform 104. The platform is located 1.80 m. north of Wall 107, the south wall of the room. The platform is made up of two lines of small stones separated by a clay filling and ending in a rectangular block 0.75 x 0.50 m. The threshold block in Wall 101 from which the platform projects was cut back to accommodate the platform.
North of platform 104, 4.00 m. north of Wall 107 and 1.40 m. east of Wall 101, is a second platform or Counter 103. This free-standing platform or counter, 1.50 long x 0.46 wide x 0.46 m. high, is made up of two courses of large marés blocks on a footing. Between Counter 103 and Platform 104 to the south there is a rectangular lower

---

[7] For the presence of such upper floors or lofts in Roman shops see R. Ulrich 1996.

area in the pavement of Room V at depth 2.93, measuring 2.20 north to south x 2.70 m. east to west. This lower pavement area may have been used as a separate work space at the entrance to Room V. It is bound on the south by Platform 104 and on the north by Counter 103, both of which may have served as work benches or display counters. Just north of the east end of counter 103 there was a rectangular block, 0.26 x 0.23 m., with a square cutting in its center. This block, when found, was clearly out of position. But its original location is marked by a rectangular break in the pavement centered 0.30 m. west from the southwest corner of counter 103. The function of the small block is uncertain.

The latest floor of Room V is of beaten earth at a consistent depth of 2.70 to 2.75. It declines slightly from the south side of the room to the north side. The pavement is dark beaten clay, built up in thin layers which can be seen in section. In the sunken work area between Platforms 103 and 104 there is an especially smooth and hard clay surface at depth 2.93.

In the sounding excavated in 1995 at the southwest corner of Room V it was possible to identify three distinct pavements or floors in the room The latest floor with a distinct burnt layer over it at depth 2.73 to 2.74 is described above. It is the surface on which Room V collapsed. Beneath this floor between levels 2 and 3 in the sounding was a second floor at depth 2.77 to 2.79 marked by a distinct line of humus. On this floor a coin of Claudius was found. It, therefore, seems to date no later than the middle of the first century A.D. From the pottery evidence it may be dated to the end of the first century B.C. or the beginning of the first century A.D. The lowest floor was at depth 2.85 to 2.86 between levels 4 and 5. It was on this surface that the west wall of the room was built. Pottery evidence seems to date the floor to the first half of the first century B.C. Pottery in level 4 over this floor was three fragments of black combed ware, one fragment of Pompeian red ware, four fragments of fine-walled pottery, and six fragments of Roman common pottery. Beneath this floor was the deep foundation trench for Wall 101 with many amphora and Roman common pottery fragments in it.

Destruction fill above the latest floor was reddish earth mixed with clay and many roof tile fragments. Directly over the floor throughout the room there was a layer of crumbly burnt mud brick, 0.05 m. deep, which broke cleanly from the floor surface. At the base of the free-standing Block 100 on its north side there was a section of pinkish *opus signinum* pavement which seemed to have been set in place at floor level, 2.74. In the destruction fill west of the block and also just east of the west entrance 0.20 to 0.40 m. above the floor of the room were several large broken sections of this same pavement. Approximately 2.50 m. south southeast of block 100 there was a mass of broken roof tiles embedded in dark red mud brick over loose rubble. Pottery in the destruction fill and in the burnt layer over the floor of the room was mainly north African *terra*

sigillata Africana A and C, north African common ware, and Roman common pottery, all dating to the second half of the third century A.D.

In the center of the room, 3.50 m. from the west side and 2.00 m. north from Wall 107 there was a circular iron frame, 0.48 in diameter x 0.05 m. deep, with two rectangular iron handles, 0.20 x 0.12 m. The frame held a round ceramic bowl. In the bowl and around the frame were fragments of what seemed to be glass scoria or slag. Similar fragments of glass scoria were found on the floor of the room north and east of Block 100. The iron frame and bowl were sunk into the latest floor of the room, resting perhaps on a lower pavement at depth 2.81.

Immediately northeast of the north handle of the circular iron frame was a square, 0.52 x 0.50 m., of fine white charcoal ash. The ashes were in a shallow pit framed by pieces of cement pavement and mud bricks set on the floor of the room. A similar rectangular ash pit, 0.49 x 0.34 m., was located 0.50 m. east of the circular iron frame. This pit was ca. 0.10 m. deep, framed by mud bricks set on the floor of the room.

Piled against the north side of Wall 107 southwest from the circular iron frame was a great quantity of washed white sand. The sand was heaped 0.52 m. high against the wall over an area 2.50 east to west x 0.60 m. south to north. Immediately north of the sand pile was a deep round hole, 0.34 m. in diameter, full of sand. Note also that an amphora in Room X contained white sand. The ash pits, the white sand, and the glass scoria all suggest that glass was either molded or blown in the southern half of Room V.

Some 190 objects were found directly on the floor of the room or a short distance above. Among the more significant objects are the following:

Along the east side of the room:

An iron spoked wheel, ca. 1.20 to 1.30 m. in diameter. Two sections of the iron tire rim, 0.37 and 0.40 m. long were found together with five spokes, 0.38 to 0.40 m. long, and a section of the iron axle, 0.46 m. long. The wheel was lying on the floor of the room near the southeast corner of the room.

An iron saw, 0.80 long x 0.15 m. wide. The saw was found upside down bent against Wall 108, 0.47 m. above the floor of the room. It may have fallen from the loft above or a shelf.

A bronze brooch or pendant, an iron key with a ring handle, two short iron knife blades, a bone pin with an incised cube head, a handle and fragments of a blue glass vase.

An amphora found leaning against Wall 108 near its north end.

A small bronze frying pan, 0.18 m. in diameter with a handle 0.125 m. long, found on the floor of the room.

Three bronze coins, one of Decius (249-251 A.D.), one of Gordian III dating to 239 A.D., and one of Annia Lucilla dating to 183 A.D., all found lying on the floor of the room.

Two disk lamps, one complete and the other slightly damaged, found in destruction fill 0.60 m. above the floor.

A large bronze frying pan, trapezoidal in shape, 0.36 x 0.28 m. with a handle 0.22 m. long. The bottom of the pan was repaired with riveted bronze plates.

In the center of the room north of the free-standing Block 100:

An amphora standing upright against the low mud brick wall between the free-standing block and the wall.

A round bronze pan, 0.28 m. in diameter, found 0.20 m. above the floor at the northwest corner of the free-standing block.

Three spokes from an iron wheel.

A lead pointing tool, 0.185 m. long, square in section. Used in glass molding?

Two bronze coins, one of Marcus Aurelius (161-180 A.D.) and the other not attributable.

A bronze eyelet, two bronze finger rings, a small lead hook, a bronze pin, and several fragments of scrap iron among the smaller finds together with bits of glass scoria. In the center of the room west of the free-standing block: An iron ring, 0.07 m. in diameter, perhaps from the circular iron frame, found at the northwest corner of the second ash pit.

A second round bronze pan, 0.28 m. in diameter, found in destruction fill 0.46 m. above the floor west of the free-standing block.

Three bronze coins, one a sestertius of Philip (243-249 A.D.) found 0.46 m. above the floor west of the block.

Among the smaller finds a bronze belt buckle, a bronze bucket handle, and a round bronze plate with two bronze nails in it.

In the center of the room south of the round iron frame and the ash pits:
A bronze knife blade, 0.06 m. long

An iron ax head or fitting along with many cone-shaped bronze points found just north of Wall 107 at the break in the wall.

A second lead pointing tool, 0.125 m. long, square in section, similar to the one found further north in the room.

Among the smaller finds were two bronze nails, a flat bronze disk, 0.10 m. in diameter, a bronze knob, 0.035 in diameter x 0.023 m. tall, two bronze plates, one rectangular and the other heart-shaped, many flat iron plates, and several iron nails.

South and southeast from the free-standing block:

A hoard of 42 coins found scattered on the floor of the room to 0.40 m. above the floor in destruction fill. The latest of them is a coin of Valerian (253-260 A.D.), the earliest of Marcus Aurelius. The largest number comes from the reign of Gordianus III (238-244 A.D.). See Mattingly below p. 60.

A stone mill for grinding grain, 0.32 m. in diameter. The top and bottom stones of the mill are unbroken. The upper surface of the top stone is concave and has a butterfly-shaped cutting at its center to hold the turning mechanism. The top surface of the bottom stone is convex. To reduce its weight, the bottom of the lower stone is concave.

A very small ivory die, 0.008 m.[3] The dots on the die were made with a circular punch. It was found on the floor between the free-standing block and mud brick Wall 101.

An amphora with 58 iron nails, one bronze nail, and a triangular iron plate, found 0.16 m. above the floor.

At the south west corner of the room east from Wall 101:

The bronze base, iron stem, and bronze flower-shaped candleholder from a candelabra together with a curved iron pin for holding the candle.

A flat circular lead ring, 0.08 m. in diameter, with a rectangular handle and five perforations around a raised central knob. The function of this object is uncertain.

Two flat iron bars and two flat bronze plates.

Six large irregular pieces of scrap bronze and many irregular pieces of scrap iron.

In the rectangular work space at a lower level between platform 104 and counter 103 at the west die of the room:

A small bronze statuette of the god Mercury, 0.068 m. tall, very well preserved. (Fig. 3.11) The figure is nude with a mantle hanging over his left arm. In his right hand he holds his money bag. He is wearing a winged helmet and winged sandals. The pose is Greek. The statuette was found partially under the threshold at the south end of the entrance to the room.

Fig. 3.11 Bronze statuette of Mercury

Five bronze points and two iron fragments.

Several small fragments of bronze, iron, and lead. The lead piece is a small scoop or spoon, 0.05 x 0.023 m.

U-shaped bronze strip, 0.038 x 0.035 m.

Iron ring, 0.035 m. in diameter.

Bronze ring, 0.02 m. in diameter, very well preserved.

Bronze, iron, and lead fragments including one lead point, 0.065 m. long.

Small iron scoop, 0.07 x 0.055 m.

Iron bar, 0.19 m. long. One end is flattened and enlarged. Also a square iron ring, 0.055 x 0.055 m.

Cylindrical iron bar, 0.166 x 0.025 m. in diameter.
Iron *falx* or sickle, 0.16 x 0.05 m. Also a flat iron fragment 0.06 x 0.053 m.

Ceramic ring, 0.03 m. tall, with grooved decoration and a bored hole, possibly for holding hair in place.

Flat iron bar 0.07 m. long.

Flat bronze plate, 0.088 x 0.02 m.

Iron bar, 0.165 x 0.055 x 0.03 m.

An iron ax or hoe, 0.13 x 0.075 m.

An iron scoop or small shovel, 0.14 x 0.13 m.

A large conch shell worked at one end.

An iron bar or handle, 0.105 x 0.07 x 0.03 m.
A bronze jug, 0.20 m. tall, with a trefoil lip.

A bronze bowl, 0.25 in diameter x 0.14 m. tall. The bottom of the bowl is missing.

A flat iron plate, 0.18 x 0.16 m.

An iron *falx*, 0.305 m. long, found at the south face of Counter 103.

An iron point, 0.12 m. long. A spear point? Found next to the *falx* on the lower pavement.

Two bronze vases, one with a swing handle, the other jug-shaped.

A round bronze candelabra base and iron candelabra stem.

A narrow iron rake. The last four items were found at the south face of Counter 103.

The variety, location, and number of objects found in Room V suggest that the room was used for storage and industrial purposes. At the center of the room north of Wall 107 glass may have been molded or blown, as the sand, the glass scoria, and the ash pits suggest. In the lower rectangular work space at the entrance on the west side of the room bronze and iron may have been worked and sold, as the many iron tools and fragments of scrap bronze and iron indicate. The east side of the room may have been used for storage. There the iron wheel, the saw, three fry pans, the two disk lamps, the stone mill, the amphora with nails, and the 42 coins were found. These items may have been sitting on shelves along the mud brick Wall 101 or Wall 108.

3.4 The East Unit

The East Unit in its final phase is made up of five rooms: U1, U2, Q, T, and R. (Fig. 3.1) The unit measures overall 12.00 m. north to south x 9.30 m. west to east. The latest floors and walls of the unit are at a higher level than those of the west unit at depth 2.14-2.35 as compared to depth 2.60-2.70 m. in the west unit. The east unit is at roughly the same level as the floor of the forum and the shops along the west side of the forum (2.05 to 2.15 m.). The unit is, however, independent, not connected to the forum shops except perhaps by way of Room T. The east wall of that room may have been destroyed by the earlier excavators. The entrance to the east unit in its final phase was from the north into Room U1. There was perhaps a street running east to west along the north side of the complex, but the evidence for that street was removed by a trench of the earlier excavators or the construction of the late defensive wall.

3.4.1 Room U

Stratigraphic soundings at the north end of Room U2 and along Wall 19108 indicate that in the earliest phase of the East Unit there was a single large Room U, measuring 4.00 m. west to east x 5.90 m. south to north. This earlier room was bound on the east by Wall 19108, on the south by the well and Wall 107, and on the west by Wall 20108. There is only the slightest evidence of a north wall which may have been destroyed by later construction along the north side of the unit or by the earlier excavators. In a sounding at the north end of Wall 20108 there was a single large block lying north of the wall and perpendicular to it at depth 3.31. This block may belong to the footing of the north wall of the complex.

In the sounding at the north end of Wall 20108 it was learned that the wall was constructed by filling a deep trench at depth 3.04 with leveling stones on which the ashlar courses of the wall were laid. The lowest ashlar course of the wall is at depth 2.77. But on the east side the course just above the lowest course at depth 2.62 projects outward from the wall as though it was meant to serve as a footing for the wall on this side. Examination of the stratigraphy in connection with the wall seems to establish that the wall was constructed on a surface at depth 2.77. Pottery recovered beneath that surface was ten fragments of hand-made Talayotic wares, one fragment of Campanian A ware, and nine fragments of Roman Republican common pottery, all indicating a date in the first half of the first century B.C. for the construction of the wall. At a later date, perhaps in the late first century or early second century A.D., the floor level of the room was raised to depth 2.54. Pottery beneath this floor was mainly Roman common wares with four fragments of *terra sigillata Africana* A, and a modest amount of north African common wares. Finally the floor of the room was again raised in the third century A.D. to depth 2.35. It was on this latest floor that Room U2 collapsed.

In a sounding at the juncture of Walls 110 and 19108 at the southwest corner of Room T it was learned that the large reused blocks which make up Wall 110 are resting on an earlier ashlar wall. This earlier wall is almost certainly the continuation eastward from the well of Wall 107. Three regular ashlar courses of the wall remain in place at depth 2.74. Beneath them in a deep trench is a packing of leveling stones to depth 2.92. This earlier wall almost certainly butted up against the wellhead and the arch of the well as does Wall 107 west of the wellhead. Thus in its earliest phase Room U was bound on the south by Wall 107 with the well at the center of the room on its south side.

In the sounding at the southwest corner of Room T and in another sounding at the northwest corner of Room Q it was learned that there was an earlier wall as well beneath Wall 19108, the east wall of Room U1. Only one course of this lower wall remains in place at depth 2.79 to 2.84.

At its south end this wall rests on a footing of large field stones to depth 2.92 and at its north end on a packing of clay at depth 2.84. This lower wall was destroyed, and a new wall at depth 2.32 to 2.49 was built over it. At its south end the later wall rests on a packing of small stones and clay, 0.28 m. deep, over the earlier wall. At its north end the later wall rests on a leveling course of field stones set on the lower wall.

The most striking feature of Room U in its early phase was the well centered in the south wall of the room. In a sounding at the northwest corner of Room R at the juncture of Wall 107, Wall 106, and the well it was clear that Wall 107 is contemporary with the well. The bottom of the wellhead is at depth 2.76. The bottom of the lowest ashlar course of Wall 107 is at depth 2.75. Wall 107 was built up against the wellhead, and the outer surfaces of the lowest stones in the arch of the well were dressed to receive courses of the wall. The well located at the center of the south wall was clearly intended to go with Room U, not Room R to the south. It was not uncommon for the Romans to build a well into the wall of a room. As a part of the wall, the well could be approached from two different rooms.

At some point in the third century Room U was divided into two rooms, Rooms U1 and U2, by the construction of Wall 117. This wall rests on the latest floor of Room U2 at depth 2.35.

3.4.2 Room U1

Room U1, the eastern new room, became a long entrance corridor, 2.10 west to east x 5.90 m. north to south. From this corridor there is access to Room R to the south and Room U2 to the west.

The room is framed on the north by a large threshold, 2.00 x 0.68 m., made up of ten small blocks, on the east by Wall 19108, on the south by wall or threshold 111 and the arch of the well, and on the west by Wall 117.

The large north entrance threshold is complete except for a single block at its northwest corner. The top of the threshold is at depth 2.12-2.15. The threshold is worn by treading along its north side. It thus marks an impressive entrance to the east unit from the north. North of wall 117 and north of the threshold there are several very large flat blocks. The top of the southernmost of these blocks, measuring 0.90 x 0.80 m., is at depth 2.46. This stone may have been laid to support the missing north wall of Room U2. Northeast of this block is a second block, 0.95 x 0.95 m., at depth 2.56. The top of this second block is at depth 2.40. East of it is a third block, and on top of it is still another large block, 0.60 x 0.60 m. at depth 2.25. On top of this last block at depth 2.25 was a layer of cement, and above the cement layer there was originally a tile pavement. One tile from this pavement remains in place against the threshold into Room U1. The function of these large blocks is uncertain, but they seem to have served in part as a solid foundation for a tile pavement at the entrance to Room U1. They are in line with four large blocks north of Room Q.

The east wall of the room, Wall 19108, is constructed out of regular courses of small marés blocks bonded with mud or clay. At its north end it is 0.76 m. high in three courses, at its south end 0.43 m. high above the latest floor. This upper wall was built at the level of the latest floors of Rooms Q. and T. At its south end it butts up against wall 110, the south wall of Room T. To the north it ends at the threshold in a built corner from which Wall 112, the north wall of Room Q, runs eastward.

The most prominent feature of the south side of the room is the arch of the well which served as the south wall of Room U1. From the arch Wall 107 runs off to the west. East of the arch is a single block at depth 2.04 which may have served as the threshold of a doorway from Room U into Room R. The doorway, if there was one, is 0.80 m. wide. South of the doorway were two marés blocks set into the floor of Room R and marking perhaps the approach to the doorway from that room. East of the doorway is the large westernmost block of Wall 110. It is to be noted that there is no positive indication that after the division of Room U in the third century a wall ran eastward from the top of the arch of the well as does wall 107 to the west. Several large stones including a fragment of a column base were found lying in the well under the arch and standing on end along the north side of the arch. It did not appear, however, from the position of the stones that the arch had been filled in to form a closed stone wall west of the doorway. But when Room U1 was planned, the top course of the wellhead north of the arch was removed to the level of the floor of the room. It is probable that at this stage the well had ceased to be functional and was filled in. It is also likely in spite of the lack of evidence that the space under and around the arch was filled in with mud bricks to present a solid south wall to the room with a doorway east of the arch.

The west wall of Room U1, Wall 117, is very poorly preserved. The wall stands only 0.10 m. high from the floor of Room U2, and the top of the wall is at the level of the floor of Room U1. Only a few blocks of the lowest course in the middle of the wall have survived. There are also three blocks at its north end where it meets the threshold. The wall seems, however, to have been broken by a trench of the earlier excavators at its north end. At its south end stands a large door jamb block placed over the west side of the wellhead and against Wall 107 for which it also seems to serve as a buttress. There are two doorways in the wall, one 0.80 m. wide, north of the door jamb block and the other, 0.90 m. wide, near the north end of the wall southwest from the large threshold. These doors lead into Room U2.

The latest floor of Room U1 on which the room collapsed is of beaten earth at depth 2.16 to 2.20. This floor was built up in two layers of beaten earth separated by a layer of clay. It runs through the north doorway in Wall 117 into Room U2 and over the southwest corner of the threshold. This beaten earth floor was laid over an earlier floor of ceramic *tesserae* set in clay to form a pavement. This *tessera* pavement has been exposed only in an area, 2.10 east to west x 2.00 m. south to north from the wellhead. In that area it is at depth 2.23-2.25. The pavement is adjusted with a slight gap to the top of the wellhead. It, however, runs up against the north side of door jamb Block 112 and through the south doorway into Room U2. It is certain that the door jamb block was in place before the ceramic pavement was laid. Because after exposure to the sun the *tessera* pavement is easily broken by traffic, it was exposed only in the southern third of the room. It seems probable, however, that it lies beneath the beaten earth floor throughout the room. Both the beaten earth floor and the *tessera* floor date to the third century.

Over the beaten earth floor was a layer of burnt mud brick, 0.05-0.08 m. deep. This burnt layer was more apparent in the northern half of the room than in the southern half north of the well. Above the burnt mud brick was a deep layer of destruction fill, reddish earth mixed with mud brick and clay. At the northeast corner of the room the destruction fill was dark red mud brick with many roof tile fragments in it. Pottery in the destruction fill and the burnt layer over the floor was *terra sigillata Africana* A and C, north African common wares, and Roman common pottery dating to the second half of the third century A.D.

Found lying on the beaten earth floor of the room were the following objects of interest:

A hand-made ceramic bowl, dark red in color, with a molded rim decorated with a vine motif. The shape, texture of the fabric, and decoration of this bowl are distinctive. It was found in the middle of the room next to the ten glass paste disks.

Ten circular blue glass paste disks, 0.03-0.035 m. in diameter. (Fig. 3.12) Seven of the disks have yellow and black inlay in the blue field. Three of the disks join and contain the figure of a fish swimming right. (Fig. 3.13) Parts of other fish are inlaid on other disks. The disks seem to have been cut from a flat piece of blue glass paste on which fish were portrayed swimming in a blue sea. The disks may originally have been in the hand-made bowl. They may have served as counters of some sort or pieces in a game.

A sestertius of Hadrian found just south of the large threshold.

Over the *tessera* pavement the following items were found:

A round bronze disk with a central hole, perhaps the foot of a candelabra.

Fig. 3.12 Ten blue-glass paste disks

Fig. 3.13 Fish swimming right

Two lamps, one a disk lamp unbroken and the other a disk lamp with four mouths also unbroken. The second lamp may have a stamp on its bottom.

A bronze coin, not attributable, found with the two lamps.

A bronze furniture fitting with a bronze nail or rivet and wood fragments in it.

An iron ax with several iron nails.

Several pieces of painted stucco or plaster from a wall.

3.4.3 Room U2

Room U2 to the west of Room U1 measures 5.90 north to south x 1.40 m. east to west. It is bound on the east by Wall 117, on the south by Wall 107, and on the west by Wall 20108. The north wall of the room was destroyed perhaps by a trench of the earlier excavators. There are two doorways into the room, one near the north end of Wall 117 and the other at the south end of the wall.

Wall 117 was built at the level of the latest floor of Room U2. It is only one course high at its north end and in the center. Wall 107 in this room is 0.90 m. high above the latest floor at the door jamb block dropping to 0.49 m. at the southwest corner of the room where Wall 108 meets it. Wall 108 in this room is made up of five courses of marés blocks bonded by mud or clay. It stands 0.60 m. high above the latest floor of the room.

The latest floor of Room U2 is of beaten earth at a consistent depth of 2.32-2.35. There is evidence that the *tessera* pavement of Room U1 extended through the south doorway into Room U2. Only a small patch of that pavement remains at depth 2.24. There were signs of burning over the pavement in the center of the room and along Wall 108 opposite the south doorway. Along that wall ca. 1.50 north from Wall 107 there was a deep circle of burnt mud brick and carbonized wood with a large piece of folded carbonized cloth in it. A sizable sample of the carbonized wood and cloth was collected for analysis. The carbonized wood may have come from a wooden box holding the cloth. It is possible that the deep circle of burnt mud brick resulted from the burning of tree roots. Above the patches of burning at floor level the fill in the room was typical destruction fill, reddish earth mixed with mud brick and clay. Pottery over the floor of the room and in the deep destruction fill was *terra sigillata Africana* A and C, north African common pottery, and Roman common pottery dating to the second half of the third century A.D.

Beneath this latest beaten earth floor was another beaten earth floor at depth 2.54. Over it was a fine coating of ashes along with much pottery, mainly Roman and north African common wares dating to the third century A.D. Beneath this floor is a fill of yellow earth, 0.23 m. deep, with bits of carbon in it. This fill in turn rests on a surface at depth 2.77. It was in relation to this lowest surface that Wall 108 was constructed. Pottery in the yellow earth stratum, Roman common wares together with four fragments of *terra sigillata Africana* A and a modest amount of African common pottery near the top of the fill, suggests that the floor level of Room U2 was raised to depth 2.54 in the first century A.D. and then to depth 2.35 in the late second or early third century A.D.

Directly on the latest beaten earth floor of the room or slightly above it were the following objects of interest:

An amphora, broken, found in a patch of burning in the center of the room.

Two bronze coins, one of Marcia Otacilia, wife of Philip, dating to 248 A.D. and one of Hadrian.

At Wall 108 1.50 m. north from Wall 107 in carbonized mud brick slightly above the floor of the room the following items were found:

Two disk lamps, one with an inscription scratched on its bottom.

A bronze hook, the end of a balance arm, together with four links of a bronze chain perhaps also from the balance.

A bronze *balsamarium* in the shape of a female head together with its stand.

A bronze seal stamp ring, 0.065 x 0.03 m., in the shape of an eagle with the word ACTIACI written right to left in the upper register and a legionary standard on its side left to right in a lower register. (Fig. 3.14) On the back of the stamp is the ring handle with a star on top. The designation "Actiacus" refers to a veteran of the battle of Actium or his descendant.

Fig. 3.14 ACTIACI seal stamp ring

An iron arrow head, the only arrow head found thus far at Pollentia.

A large lead box, 0.30 x 0.215 x 0.21 m., with a circular hole, 0.115 m. in diameter, on its top and the figure of bull and head of a horned deity stamped in relief on its front. The box is made from a large piece of lead folded to form the box with a second piece as the top.[8]

A bronze coin, not attributed.

Many flat pieces of iron which may be fittings from a wooden chest.

All of these objects were found together on the east side of Wall 108 at the south end of the room. The east facade of the wall was damaged for a distance of 1.00 m. in the area of these finds perhaps by the digging of a hole for an almond tree.

Wall 108 is not only the west wall of Room U2. It also served as the wall separating the west unit from the east unit. It is not clear to what use Room U2 was put. But it seems to have served chiefly as a storage room in connection with entrance corridor Room U1. Hence the lead box, the wooden chest, the balance, *balsamarium*, and the ACTIACI stamp found in the south third of the room.

3.4.4 Room Q

Room Q at the northeast corner of the unit measures 2.65 m. north to south and has been excavated to distance of 3.50 m. west to east. It is bound on the south by Wall 110, on the west by Wall 108, and on the north by Wall 112. The east side of the room lies beyond the excavated area.

Only one block of Wall 110 remains in place at the southwest corner of the room. It seems to be a door jamb block on the west side of a doorway, 0.80 m. wide, from Room Q into Room T to the south. The wall is late, dating to the third century A.D. The southeast corner of the door jamb block lies over the *dolium* at the northwest corner of Room T. At a distance 4.10 m. east from this block in Square J-18 is another block which may have survived the destruction of the wall. At the northeast corner of Square I-19 north of the line of the wall there was a row of ten fallen mud bricks resting on top of destruction debris 0.40 m. above the floor of the room. Whether these mud bricks came from wall 110 or the east wall of the room could not be ascertained.

Wall 108, the west wall of the room, is made up of three courses of marés blocks bonded by mud or clay. It survives only to a height of 0.43 m. above the latest floor of the room. The bottom of the wall is at depth 2.49. The three ashlar courses of the wall were laid over a leveling course of large field stones. They in turn rest on a lower, earlier wall at depth 2.68. Only one course of this earlier lower wall remains in place on a packing of clay at depth 2.84.[9]

Like the south wall the north wall of the room, Wall 112, is also poorly preserved. Only four blocks from its lowest course remain in place. The most prominent of them is a large rectangular block at depth 2.45 at the northwest corner of the room. This block rests on a leveling course of large field stones placed in a deep trench to depth 2.68. Wall 112, therefore, dates to the second or latest phase of Room Q. West of the corner block is a gap, 1.00 m. wide, in which there are two smaller stones which seem to be displaced. Whether this gap represents a doorway into the room from the north is uncertain. But north of the gap outside the room are three very large blocks, 0.58 x 0.80, 0.58 x 1.06, 0.60 x 1.80 m., lying flat to form either a pavement or the bedding for a pavement at depth 2.15 which may represent the level of the north street. The actual purpose of the blocks needs further study. There is a pavement of similar large blocks in the area south of the East temple or monument east of the Capitolium in Square I-11.[10]

The latest floor of Room Q is of beaten earth at a consistent depth of 2.37-2.40. The floor has been

---

[8] For the lead box, the *balsamarium*, the ACTIACI seal stamp ring, and the glass paste disks found in Room U1 see A. Arribas and N. A. Doenges 1995.

[9] For the wall see Room U above, p. 39.

[10] M. Orfila associates these blocks with the late defensive wall running east to west north of the Capitolium and the shop *insula*. See below pp. 57-58.

preserved along the west side of the room east of Wall 108. In the eastern half of the room the floor may have been broken through by a trench of the earlier excavators. There were signs of burning in the room only over the floor immediately east of Wall 108. In the western half of the room the fill over the pavement was typical destruction fill, reddish earth mixed with mud brick and clay. At the northwest corner of the room the fill was more compact dark red mud brick with many roof tile fragments in it. In the eastern half of the room the fill was loose gray earth in which there was a mass of pottery, 540 fragments of Islamic water jugs (Rosselló type 3A) and two fragments of Rosselló type 3C jugs. Nearly all of the fragments were of bases, suggesting that they came from the clearing of a well.[11] At the bottom of the gray earth were many field stones. It seems that a trench or refuse pit was dug in the period of Islamic settlement at Alcudia through the east side of Room Q. The outline of this trench is apparent in section along the east side of Square J-19. The bottom of the pit broke through the floor the room.

There was a lack of significant archaeological material other than the Islamic water jugs either in the destruction fill or directly on the floor of Room Q. In this respect Room Q was unique within the complex. Recovered was only a coin of Alexander Severus lying against the north face of Wall 112 outside the room itself. This dearth of materials suggests that much of the area of the room had been disturbed during the Islamic period and by a trench of the earlier excavators.

In a sounding at the juncture of Walls 108 and 112 at the northwest corner of the room three strata were identified. Stratum 1, the latest floor of the room, is loose gray earth from depth 2.43 to 2.55. Stratum 2 is yellowish sandy earth from depths 2.55 to 2.75. Stratum 3 is red loose earth which breaks into small chunks from depths 2.75 to 2.84. Directly below lower Wall 19108 there was a single fragment of hand-made Talayotic pottery. In stratum 1 there were eight fragments of Roman common pottery. In stratum 3 were three fragments of Iberian ware, three fragments of fine wall ware, one fragment of *terra sigillata Africana* A, one Ebusitan amphora fragment, three Roman amphora fragments, and five fragments of Roman common wares. Below depth 2.84 there was no pottery.

From the evidence of the sounding it appears that lower Wall 108 was constructed in relation to a surface at depth 2.75. Pottery in stratum 3 and beneath the wall would date its construction to the first century B.C. On the evidence from Room T the ground level in the area of the room was raised to depth 2.55 when the lower wall was built or shortly thereafter. Still later but perhaps in the late second or early third century A.D. the ground level in the room was again raised to depth 2.37- 2.43. When this latest floor was laid, lower Wall 108 was destroyed,

and a new wall was constructed at the higher level. It was at this point that the area east of Wall 108 and north of Wall 107, the lower south wall of Room T, was divided into Rooms Q and T. The evidence of the lower walls suggests that before the construction of the two rooms in the third century A.D. the area they occupy was open ground.

3.4.5 Room T

Room T south of Room Q measures 2.65 m. north to south and has been excavated to a distance of 3.40 m. west to east. It is bound on the north by Wall J19110, on the west by Wall 108, and on the south by Wall 19110/101. No east wall of the room has been identified. The room, indeed, seems to continue eastward into Square I-18 without apparent interruption to the rear wall of Room P.

Only one block of Wall J19110 remains in place at the northwest corner of the room. A second block 4.10 m. to the west in Square J-18 may also belong to this wall. At the northwest corner of the room there may have been a doorway, 0.80 m. wide, between Room Q and Room T. The bedding for a threshold or the continuation of the wall was apparent east of the block at the northwest corner of the room. Wall J19110 is late, dating to the latest phase of Room T. The single remaining block of the wall rests on top of the north *dolium* found in 1993 along the west side of the room.

Wall 108, the west wall of the room, is made up three courses of marés blocks bonded by mud or clay. It stands only 0.46 m. high above the latest floor of the room. At its south end Wall 108 ends before it meets Wall 110/101, the south wall of the room. The bottom of the ashlar courses of the wall is at depth 2.32. Thus the wall was constructed in relation to the latest floor of Room T. This wall rests on a packing of clay and stones, 0.28 m. deep, over a lower, earlier wall along the same line as the upper wall. Only one course of the lower wall remains in place at depth 2.79 at the southwest corner of the room. This lower wall rests on a deep footing of large field stones to depth 2.92. It butts up against Wall 107, the lower, earlier south wall of the room.

Wall 110/101 at its west end is made up of two large reused blocks, one 0.87 x 0.53 m. and the other 0.74 x 0.58 m., both lying at the level of the latest floor of the room. At its east end is a door jamb block, 101, which marks the west end of Wall 102. The door jamb block, 101, was added on to Wall 102 with which it is not in line to make the doorway from Room T into Room R. The doorway is 0.90 m. wide. Four thin stones from the broken threshold of the doorway were found in place. The two large reused blocks of Wall 110 are uncharacteristically wide as compared to Walls 102 and 108, as though they replaced a wall of normal width. They, indeed, rest on an earlier lower wall which almost certainly is the continuation of Wall 107 east of the well. Three regular ashlar courses of the lower wall remain in

---

[11] Orfila, M. and Riera, M. 2002. Sixty fragments of Islamic jugs were also found in destruction fill over Room T.

place at depth 2.74. Beneath them in a deep trench is a packing of leveling stones to depth 2.92. This earlier wall almost certainly butted up against the wellhead and the arch of the well as does Wall 107 west of the wellhead. The top course of the earlier wall was cut back to accommodate the eastern reused block of wall 110. Thus the lower wall was still partially standing when wall 110 at the level of the latest floor of Room T was laid on top of it.

The latest floor of Room T is of beaten earth at a consistent depth of 2.32-2.35. Over the floor there was a shallow layer of burnt mud brick, 0.05 m. deep, especially conspicuous along the east side of Square I-19. Along the south side of the room above the burnt layer the fill was reddish earth mixed with mud brick and clay. Pottery in this fill was *terra sigillata Africana* A and C, north African common wares, and Roman common pottery dating to the second half of the third century A.D. Along the north side of the room the fill was gray loose earth with many stones and fragments of roof tiles in it but little pottery. It is possible that the area of gray fill represents a trench of the earlier excavators which ran west to east in the northern half of the room. In digging the trench the excavators may have destroyed most of Wall J19110.

In a sounding at the southwest corner of the room four strata were identified including the latest floor. Stratum 1, the latest floor of the room, is gray loose earth, from depths 2.36 to 2.58. Stratum 2 is reddish crumbly earth with much clay from depths 2.58 to 2.92. Stratum 3 is red earth which breaks into small clumps from depths 2.92 to 2.95. Stratum 4 is black burnt earth or mud brick, from depths 2.95 to 3.01. On this surface there was a bedding of flat stones on which the leveling stones for the lower walls rest. Beneath stratum 4 there was no pottery. Pottery in stratum 1 included two fragments of hand-made Talayotic ware, six fragments of Iberian pottery, four fragments of fine wall ware, one fragment of Campanian B, one fragment of *terra sigillata Gallica*, two fragments of *terra sigillata Africana* A, three Ebusitan amphora fragments, and forty-five fragments of Roman common wares, all suggesting that the fill of the latest floor of the room was taken from a mixed Roman deposit. Pottery in stratum 2 was one fragment of Campanian A, eight Roman amphora fragments, and two fragments of Roman common wares. Pottery in stratum 3 was five Roman amphora fragments and two Ebusitan amphora fragments. In stratum 4 the pottery was one fragment of hand-made Talayotic ware, three Roman amphora fragments, one Ebusitan amphora fragment, and three fragments of Roman common wares.

At depth 2.46 in the sounding at the southwest corner of the room was a roof tile embedded in plaster and set at an angle to wall 108, 0.20 m. east from the wall. The roof tile may have served as a base on which was placed an altar or table. Along the west side of the room north of the roof tile and also 0.20 m. east from the wall were two half *dolia*, 0.55 m. in diameter. (Fig. 3.15) The *dolia*

like the roof tile were embedded in a floor or surface at depth 2.46. The south *dolium* held seventy fragments of a distinctive Roman green glaze crater along with four fragments of Roman common ware. The bowl has been restored. (Fig. 3.16) In the north *dolium* were one fragment of fine wall pottery, twelve Roman amphora fragments, eight fragments of Roman common ware, and two fragments of north African common pottery. The north *dolium* lies partly under door jamb block J19110. The roof tile and the dolia were covered over when the latest pavement was laid in Room T and the upper Walls 108 and 110 were constructed.

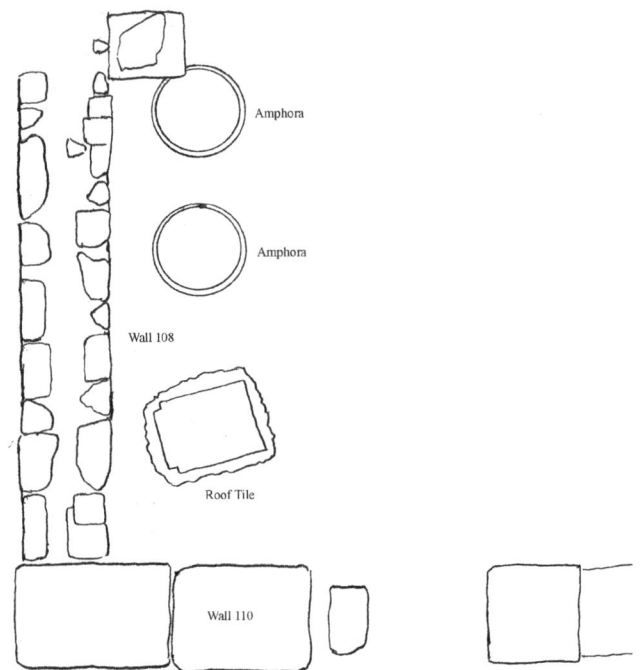

Fig. 3.15 Roof tile and two dolia embedded in first century A.D. surface of Room T.

Fig. 3.16 Green glass crater from the south dolium in Room T.

From the evidence of the sounding it appears that Wall 107 and lower Wall 108 were constructed on a surface at depth 2.75 in the first century B.C. But perhaps when the wall was built or shortly thereafter the ground level east of Wall 108 was raised to depth 2.55-2.58. Later but perhaps in the late first century B.C. or early first century A.D. the ground level was raised again to depth 2.46. It is on this surface that the roof tile was laid and the two *dolia* were sunk. Then perhaps in the late second or early third century A.D. the latest floor was put down at depth 2.32-2.36. At the same time upper wall 108 replaced lower wall 108 which was destroyed and wall 110 out of reused blocks was built over wall 107 along the south side of the room. Only then was the area east of wall 108 and north of wall 107 divided into Rooms Q and T.

On the latest floor of Room T especially along the east side of the room there were the following objects of interest:

Two bronze coins, one of Gordian III and the other of Philip.

A round bronze disk, perhaps the base of a candelabra.

A small bronze figurine of a draped seated figure. (Fig. 3.17)

Fig. 3.17 Bronze statuette of seated figure.

A T-shaped bronze fitting perhaps from a wooden box or furniture.

Two iron keys very well preserved.

A pyramid-shaped lead weight.

A bronze coiled snake found lying against wall 102. It served as a handle or attachment. (Fig. 3.18)

Beneath Rooms Q and T there was in an earlier phase a large open area, measuring 5.92 south to north at depth 2.55. Its dimension west to east has not been determined. This space was bound on the west by lower Wall 108 and on the south by Wall 107 running east from the well. Its east boundary may have been the rear wall of Room P. As there was no wall beneath Wall 112, the north wall of

Room Q, it seems that the area was open to the north. It corresponds in size to Room V in the west unit of the Dartmouth complex.

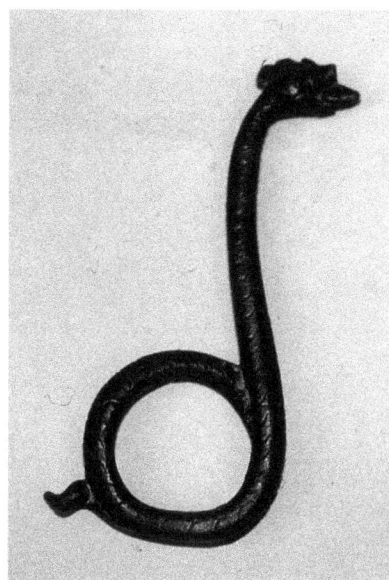

Fig. 3.18 Bronze coiled snake.

3.4.6 Room R

Room R south of Rooms T and U1 is trapezoidal in shape. It measures 4.50 m. north to south. At its south side it is 5.80 m. wide west to east, at its north side 5.50 m. wide west to east. It is bound on the north by Wall 107, the arch of the well, Threshold 111, and Wall 110; on the east by Wall 100; on the south by Wall 101; and on the west by Wall 106. In its latest phase there were two entrances into the room, one from Room T and one from Room U1.

Wall 107 runs west from the arch of the well and seems to have been built at the same time as the well. The bottom of the wellhead is at depth 2.76. The lowest ashlar course of Wall 107 is at depth 2.75. Beneath it are leveling stones in a trench to depth 2.86. In an earlier construction phase a section of Wall 107 also extended east of the well. For this section of the wall, Wall 110 laid over it in the third century, and the doorway between Room T and Room R see above pp. 43-44. For a door between Room U1 and Room R see p. 40.

Wall 100, the east wall of the room, is made up of two lower courses of large reused blocks with a third course of smaller blocks at the top. The large blocks are fitted together without a bonding of mud or clay. At least one of the large blocks is a cushioned ashlar block which may have come from the large monument base east of the Capitolium. Wall 100 was constructed initially in relation to a floor at depth 2.55 and was thus contemporary with the lower ashlar section of Wall 101, the south wall of the room. Wall 100 stands 0.97 m. high from the latest floor of Room R.

The south wall of Room R, Wall 101, was constructed from three courses of large reused blocks fitted carefully together with a thin layer of mud or clay at its west end but without mortar at the east end. At a distance of 1.25 m. from the southeast corner of the room there was originally a doorway, 1.00 m. wide. This doorway was later blocked up with four courses of small stones set in mud or clay mortar. At its east end Wall 101 is bonded with the upper courses of Wall 100. At its west end Wall 101 butts up against Wall 106. Beneath the west end of the wall at the time of excavation there was a sizable empty space which may have resulted from a hole or well which had been filled in. Over time the fill in the well may have settled with the result that the west end of the wall was found suspended above a deep empty cavern without support. The upper section of Wall 101 made up of reused blocks is 0.95 m. high. It was constructed at the level of the second floor of the room at depth 2.17. But this upper section of the wall rests directly on an earlier lower wall, three ashlar courses high, from depth 2.14 to 2.55. Beneath the ashlar courses is a deep leveling course of field stones packed in earth to depth 2.76. This lower wall is of normal thickness and construction out of small ashlar blocks bonded by mud or clay. Between the two upper ashlar courses there is a row of roof tiles

The west wall of the room, Wall 106, is in fact the east wall of Room X. It is made up of eight courses of small blocks bonded by mud or clay mortar. But these smaller blocks together with roof tile fragments were laid around three massive reused blocks set on end. On the east side of the wall there is a gap left between the southern two massive blocks. The wall is 1.38 high at its south end and 1.28 at its north end. The bottom of the wall on its east side is at depth 2.58 to 2.63. The wall is not perpendicular to Wall 107 against which it is built but angles slightly south-southwest. This wall constructed out of reused blocks and roof tiles is almost certainly late. At its south end beneath the upper section of Wall 101 there remains a small section of an earlier phase of the wall. This earlier wall is five ashlar courses high from depth 2.61. It like the lower section of Wall 101 was broken by the well or hole beneath the west end of Wall 101.

From soundings along walls 101 and 106 and in the center of the room it is possible to identify at least five pavements or surfaces in Room R. The uppermost pavement at depth 2.00 to 2.02 is of powdery gray beaten earth. This pavement in the northeast quadrant of Room R was coated with a thin layer of *sauló* or decomposed marés which hardened into a durable bright yellow surface when exposed to air. It was on this pavement that Room R collapsed. The doorway through Wall 101, later blocked, was constructed in relation to this latest floor of the room. The second pavement at depth 2.09 to 2.15, is of compact red earth with small stones or pebbles set into it. A large patch of this pebble pavement remains along the east side of the room. This pavement represents the floor level going with the upper or later

section of Wall 101. The third pavement is of beaten white clay at depths 2.32 to 2.34. Beneath the thin clay surface there is a deep layer of red loose earth to depths 2.55 to 2.58. On the clay pavement was a mass of pottery, mainly *terra sigillata Africana* A and C fragments along with north African and Roman common pottery. Similar pottery in lesser amounts was recovered on the second pavement. The fourth pavement at depths 2.55 to 2.58 is of compact yellowish red beaten earth. This pavement is the floor level going with the lower or earlier section of Wall 101 and Wall 100. The fifth pavement is also of yellowish red beaten earth with a thin layer of ashes over it at depth 2.64. It was on this pavement that the earlier section of Wall 106 was constructed. A bronze coin of Germanicus issued by the Emperor Claudius was found on this surface. Finally at depth 2.74 to 2.76 is the clay surface on which the leveling stones of Wall 101 were laid and on which Wall 107 was constructed. On this surface at Wall 106 an Iberian coin with Pegasus flying right was found and at the north face of Wall 101 at depth 2.86 there was a pyramidal lead loom weight along with hand-made Talayotic and Iberian pottery.

Pottery in strata 3 and 4 under the clay pavement but above pavement 5 was mainly Arretine or *terra sigillata Gallica* with one fragment of Campanian B ware and a few fragments of Roman and north African common wares. But in stratum 3 at depth 2.47 there was a sestertius of Antoninus Pius so that this stratum and the clay pavement may be dated to the late second or early third century A.D. The pottery would seem to date stratum 4 to the late first century B.C. or early first century A.D. Pottery in strata 5 was hand-made Talayotic ware together with fragments of Iberian and Roman Republican wares dating to the first century B.C.

The history of Room R is complex but can be tentatively reconstructed from the evidence of the soundings and the walls. The earliest structures in the area of Room R were the well and Wall 107 running west and east from the well. They were constructed in relation to the earliest surface at depths 2.75 to 2.86 on which the Iberian coin and the lead loom weight were found. The footing of Wall 107 was sunk into a stratum containing hand-made Talayotic and locally made Roman Republican common pottery dating to the first half of the first century B.C. The well and Wall 107, therefore, may be dated early in the first century B.C. At the time when the well and the wall were constructed or very shortly thereafter the ground level south of the wall was raised to depth 2.64. At this stage there was no Room R south of the well. Somewhat later perhaps toward the end of the first century B.C or early in the first century A.D. the ground level was raised to depth 2.55 to 2.58. On this beaten earth pavement the Claudian coin was found along with an almost complete Arretine bowl. It was in relation to this pavement that the lower earlier section of Wall 101 was constructed as well as early Wall 106 and the lower courses of Wall 100, the east wall of the room. Room R, therefore, dates to the end of the first century B.C. or early first century A.D. Still later but perhaps in the late second or early third century A.D. a new clay floor was laid in the room at depth 2.32 to 2.34. Wall 110 and the doorway between Room R and Room T were constructed in relation to this floor. Then at some point in the third century A.D. there seems to have been a major disturbance in the room. On the clay floor throughout the room there was a mass of north African sigillata and north African common pottery. As a result of the disturbance a new floor with a pebble surface was put down at depth 2.09 to 2.14. At the same time the upper later section of Wall 101 was built over the earlier wall, Wall 100 was raised as well, and Wall 106 was completely rebuilt. All of these later walls were constructed with reused blocks from other buildings in the Forum, evidence that the deterioration of the Forum area of Pollentia had already begun. This pebble floor was laid at the level of the top of the wellhead at the northwest corner of the room. It is thus likely that at this point, if not earlier, the well was filled in and ceased to be serviceable. Finally somewhat later in the third century the floor level was again raised to depth 2.00 to 2.02. This floor was surfaced with *sauló*. In relation to this floor a door between Room U1 and Room R may have been opened east of the arch of the well. A second door was opened through Wall 101 at the south east corner of the room. Still later this doorway through Wall 101 was blocked up. It was on the *sauló* floor or surface that the room collapsed at the end of the third century or early in the fourth century A.D.

Over the latest floor there was general destruction fill, reddish earth with mud brick and clay in it. Along the west side of the room at Wall 106 at its upper level the fill was dark red, very compact mud brick which had fallen on lighter, more clayey destruction fill. There was no evidence of destruction by fire in Room R. The shallow burnt layer found over the latest floors in the other rooms was absent in Room R. But in the northeast corner of the room there was a patch of white charcoal ashes, 0.03 deep, with many fragments of glass vases in it. At a distance 1.50 m. north of Wall 101 a trench, 1.50 m. wide, of the earlier excavators was dug through the center of the room, starting 1.50 m. east of Wall 106. The fill in this trench was loose gray earth. At the bottom of the trench were many building blocks and field stones which may have been thrown into the trench when it was refilled. The trench disturbed the stratigraphy and the floors in the center of the room.

Lying directly on the latest floor or found in the destruction fill over the floor were several Items of interest:

Six coins: an As of Emporion in fill at depth 1.50, an Antoninianus of Gallienus at depth 1.36, a follis of Constantine at depth 1.37, a sestertius of Gordian III at depth 1.36, a bronze coin, illegible, at depth 1.48, and a bronze half-coin, illegible, directly on the floor at depth 2.03.

A bronze *balsamarium* in the shape of a bell at depth 1.41

A bronze ring on the floor at depth 2.07

An iron ring, 0.05 m. in diameter, at depth 2.05

An amphora fragment inscribed with COLE/GETVA at depth 2.03

On the second pavement the following items were found:

A lead vase crushed at depth 2.14

A bronze dish or bowl also crushed at depth 2.20

A bone pin or needle at depth 2.18 along with several strips of unworked bone

On the third clay pavement an iron balance weight was found at depth 2.36

In the fill between the third and fourth pavements just east of Wall 106 a fragment of a bronze bowl and a sestertius of Antoninus Pius were found at depth 2.47. On the lowest surfaces were found the Germanicus coin of Claudius, the Iberian coin, and the lead loom weight noted above.

3.5 Summary

From the evidence of the soundings made in 1993 and 1995 it appears that the oldest structures in the Dartmouth College sector of the excavations were Rooms U, V, and Y. The earliest walls of these rooms were constructed at the same ground level. The floors and walls of the three rooms are also at roughly the same depth, 2.70-2.75. Of this early complex the most important feature is the well together with Wall 107 which ran east and west from the wellhead. It is likely that the well and the wall were constructed at the same time. The wall was built up against the wellhead and the arch of the well. The bottom of the wellhead and the lowest ashlar course of the wall are at the same depth, 2.75. While it is possible that the well existed somewhat earlier, the well and the wall clearly go together and must be roughly contemporary. Wall 107 is the key structure of the complex. All the rooms in the Dartmouth complex were laid out north or south of Wall 107.

Wall 107 along with all of the earliest walls of Rooms U, V, and Y date no earlier than the second quarter of the first century B.C. The foundation trenches of these walls were dug into strata containing mainly hand-made Talayotic pottery along with fragments of Roman Republican common wares, Campanian B pottery, and Punic or Ebusitan amphorae. The occurrence of Roman Republican and Campanian wares in strata below the surfaces going with the earliest walls suggests that there was a Roman presence on or near the site of Pollentia in the period before the first stone and mud brick buildings were constructed in the Forum area. This evidence supports the conclusion that if Q. Caecilius Metellus Balearicus established a settlement on the site of Pollentia in 123 B.C. it may have involved little more than a small group of "Romaioi" or Italians from the mainland living with natives in a post-Talayotic village. The Roman city of Pollentia dates on the archaeological evidence no earlier than the Sertorian War of 81-71 B.C. Indeed, it may have been Q. Caecilius Metellus Pius, grand nephew of Balearicus, who founded Pollentia after that war as a Latin colony. It along with Palma became a *colonia civium Romanorum* under either Caesar or Augustus.[12]

Rooms V and Y were large shops facing the West Street. Room Y like Room V may at first have been one large room extending eastward to the line of Wall 106. The counters near their wide entrances together with the statuette of Mercury found at the entrance to Room V suggest that they served as *tabernae* or shops. Room V seems to have been primarily a workshop in which glass was blown and iron and bronze was worked. Room Y may have been a tavern in which food and wine were served. In both rooms there was ample space for storage. Both rooms continued to function as workshops or *tabernae* from the first century B.C. until their collapse in the late third century A.D.

The original function of Room U facing north is less certain. The presence of the well in the middle of the south wall of the room suggests that the room had initially an industrial purpose. It is possible that in its initial phase the room was open at its north side and unroofed. There is no solid evidence of a north wall to the room at the level of the footing to Wall 20108. But at some point toward the end of the first century B.C. or early in the first century A.D. the floor level of the room was raised from depth 2.70 to depth 2.55. At the same time the ground level east of Wall 19108, the area of later Rooms T and Q, and south of Wall 107 east of Room Y was also raised to depth 2.55. It was, thus, in the Augustan period or slightly later that the higher ground level of the east unit was established. The area east of Room U between that room and the *tabernae* along the west side of the Forum may, however, have remained at this stage undeveloped.

When the ground level of the east unit was raised, Room R was constructed south of Wall 107 and the well. The earliest walls 106, 101, and 100 were built in relation to the fourth floor at depth 2.55 to 2.58. At this same time Room X was constructed at the east end of Room Y. Then at some point probably in the late second or early third century the floor level in Room R was raised to depth 2.32-2.34. This floor was paved with a coating of

compact white clay. At the same time the floor level in Room U was raised to depth 2.35. In the area east of Room U Rooms Q and T were constructed with their floors at depth 2.32 to 2.37. In adding these rooms, the builders tore down early Wall 19108, and a new Wall 108 was constructed at the higher level. Then in the early third century a new pebble floor was laid in Room R at depth 2.09-2.14, and Walls 101 and 100 were raised by setting large building blocks from other structures on top of the old walls. Wall 106 was torn down and completely rebuilt., and Room X was extensively remodeled. It was also at this point that the well in Wall 107 was filled in and Room U was divided in two with the construction of Wall 117. Room U1 became an entrance corridor facing north with a *tessera* pavement floor. Somewhat later because of its fragility that floor was covered over with a hard beaten earth surface. Perhaps at the same time in Room R a new *sauló* floor was put down at depth 2.02-2.04. Shortly thereafter Rooms Q, T, U1, U2, V, X, and Y suffered irreparable damage by fire and were abandoned. Only Room R may have survived and continued to be occupied into the fourth century.

The pottery, coins, and other articles found on the latest floors in both the west and east units indicate that the entire complex except Room R was destroyed by fire at a single point in time. The north African wares and the coins date the collapse of the structure to the second half of the third century A.D. The evidence of the coins suggests a date between 270 and 280 A.D.[13] The latest coin from the hoard in Room V is a sestertius of Valerian (253-260 A.D.). Many of the coins found directly on the latest floors are coins of Gordian III (238-244 A.D.), Philip (244-249 A.D.), or Decius Traianus (249-251 A.D.). An Antoninianus of Gallienus dating to 268 A.D. was found in destruction fill at the southwest corner of Room R. In the same area and at the same depth (1.37 m.) was a follis of Constantine. Both of these late coins are in excellent condition. If a period of ten to twenty years is allowed for the circulation of the coins found on or just above the latest pavements, a date close to 280 A.D. seems reasonable for the destruction of the complex.[14]

---

[12] See Mattingly 1983: 245-246 and note 15, and Knapp 1977: 131-139. That there was some sort of structural reorganization at Pollentia in the Augustan period can perhaps be seen in the building activity in Rooms U, Q, T. and R of the Dartmouth sector.

[13] It is significant that only nine fragments of *terra sigillata Africana D* pottery have been found in the destruction fill over the latest floors in the Dartmouth sector, two fragments in loose fill in Room T and seven on the latest floor in Room R. *Terra sigillata Africana A* pottery occurs along with *terra sigillata Africana C* in roughly equal amounts. Only in Room X is there a noticeable scarcity of these African red slip wares.

[14] H. B. Mattingly, below p. 69, notes that the latest coins are six Antoniniani of Claudius Gothicus dating to 268-270 A.D. They are followed by a single denarius of Aurelian dating to 274/5, a reform coin of Tacitus dating to 275/6, and two reform coins of Probus dating between 276 and 282 A.D. A third reform coin of Probus was found in Ca'n Viver in 1973. For a discussion of the numismatic evidence see also A. Arribas and M. Tarradell 1987.

Even before the collapse of the rooms in the Dartmouth sector, major public buildings in the Forum area of Pollentia must have fallen into disrepair, and many may have been abandoned. The latest walls in Room R and Room U, notably walls 100, 101, 110, and 106 in Room R and Wall 117 in Room U, were constructed with large reused building blocks taken from other buildings. A cushioned ashlar block in Wall 100 may have come from the large base or temple east of the Capitolium. These walls, as the pottery found in abundance on the floors associated with them indicate, date to the middle of the third century A.D. By that date the center of Pollentia had begun to decay perhaps as a result of a sharp decline in population. Economic activity may have ceased in the *tabernae* along the west side of the Forum. The shops were occupied by squatters, and rough rooms were built along the portico in front of the shops. The cause of this decay cannot be determined from the archaeological evidence. But by the middle of the third century a similar decline can be detected in many urban centers on the peninsula as well. Cities were losing population as a result of economic depression, political insecurity, and perhaps disease. At Pollentia those who remained retreated gradually to the northwest corner of the city where the large atrium houses were divided into small apartments. Before the end of the century a defensive wall was built around the inhabited area at Sa Portella, and the entire center of the city was allowed to fall into ruin. By the mid-fourth century A.D. the south, east, and north sides of the Forum were used as a burial ground. But the site of the Capitolium was respected. Indeed, the temple itself may have survived though in poor repair. In the Dartmouth sector a few small mud brick hovels with concrete floors were constructed on a different orientation from that of the earlier buildings. When they were built, the earlier shops and workrooms lay beneath a mound of rubble and mud brick. Urban life at Pollentia had come to an end.

Chapter 4

POLLENTIA EXCAVATIONS 1995-2000

4.1 Changes in leadership

Excavation of the Pollentia forum began under the co-direction of Antonio Arribas, Miguel Tarradell, and Daniel Woods, the same team which had conducted the excavations in Sa Portella. When Miguel Tarradell retired in 1989, Dra. Mercedes Roca Roumens succeeded him as Professor of Archaeology in Barcelona and co-director in Alcudia. Daniel Woods died in 1992, leaving Arribas and Dra. Roca in charge at Pollentia with Norman Doenges serving as field director of the Dartmouth College sector of the dig.

Dra. Roca resigned as co-director in the fall of 1995. To ensure continuity in the directorate of the site, Antonio Arribas appointed Dra. Margarita Orfila Pons to succeed her. At that time Dra. Orfila was *Professora Adjunta* in the Department of Prehistory and Archaeology at the University of Granada.[1] She had participated in the Forum excavations almost from their beginning in 1979, first as a field assistant and then as a specialist in Roman pottery working in collaboration with Norman Doenges. Dra. Orfila brought renewed energy, enthusiasm, and direction to the excavations. She introduced new approaches to field work and revised the system of notation and record keeping. Most importantly she brought with her a new team of field assistants. In 1997 she initiated an annual Practicum in Field Archaeology involving each summer up to twenty students from Spanish and European universities. The students are instructed in field techniques, treatment of finds, field notation, classification of pottery and coins, and cataloguing of materials. When the Bryant Foundation withdrew its funding of the Forum excavations in 1997, Dra. Orfila turned to the city of Alcudia for support. The city provides board and lodging for excavators and students in the Practicum. A consortium of four government entities[2] organized in 2000 exercises general supervision over Pollentia and provides funding for excavation and consolidation of the site.

4.2 Overview

When Dra. Orfila took over direction in the field in 1996, she centered her attention on several areas of the Forum. Her primary objective has been to define more accurately the history of the site: when and under what conditions Roman construction began, the changes which occurred from the first century B.C. to the third century A.D., the firing and destruction of the shops on the west side of the forum, the construction of a major fortification system along the north side of the forum, and in recent years her attention has turned to an elucidation of the modular plan of the city of Pollentia. Field work from 1995 to 2000 centered on Room Z and the West Street, Room A, the corridor Room B, a sounding between the shops on the west side of the Forum and the Capitolium, the late fortification wall, and a late room south of the Capitolium.

4.3 Room Z

Room Z is located directly south of Room Y and south of the narrow corridor between the two rooms. It occupies parts of Squares G-21, G-22, F-21, and F-22 in the Pollentia grid plan. Excavation of the room began in 1994 under the supervision of Norman Doenges. Dra. Orfila took over direction from Doenges in 1996 and completed investigation of the room in 2000. (Fig. 4.1)

The room is bound on the north by wall E-38, on the east by wall E-36, on the south by wall E-84, and on the west by the entrance wall E-47.[3] The north wall E-38 runs eastward 3.47 m. from wall E-47 at the northwest corner of the room. It consists of two courses of largish ashlar blocks topped toward its western end with an additional course of smaller irregularly shaped stones. The wall ends approximately 0.40 m. from the northeast corner of the room with a flat block which may have served as half of a threshold for a doorway at that corner. The block at depth 2.35 has a deep cutting, 0.25 long south to north x 0.05 m. wide, which may have held part of the wood doorframe. Four small flat stones at depths 2.48 to 2.55 immediately south of the threshold may have served as steps up to the entrance at the level of the walkway between Rooms Y and Z. The footing of wall E-38 is at depth 2.96, the top at depth 2.03.

Butting up against wall E-38 1.80 m. east from the west wall of the room is a large marés block, 0.95 east to west x 0.90 m. north to south. On the top surface of the block at depth 2.38 there were traces of cement and stucco. At the northeast corner of the block at depth 2.45 was a

[1] Dra. Orfila was appointed *Catedratica de Arqueología* in the University of Granada in October, 2000. When Antonio Arribas died October 28, 2002, she became sole director of the Pollentia excavations. The author wishes to thank Dra. Orfila for her generosity in sharing with him annual reports on the excavations each year and for responding patiently and thoughtfully to his many queries. The data in this chapter are based in part on those reports and on publications of the excavation team.
[2] *Consorci de la Ciutat Romana de Pollentia*. Participating entities are the City of Alcudia, the *Consell Insular de Mallorca*, the Balearic Government, and the Ministry of Education and Culture. See Orifla 2000: 23.

[3] See Orfila, Arribas, and Cau 1999: 104-106; Orfila, Arribas, and Doenges 1999: 91-92; and Orfila 2000: 90-103.

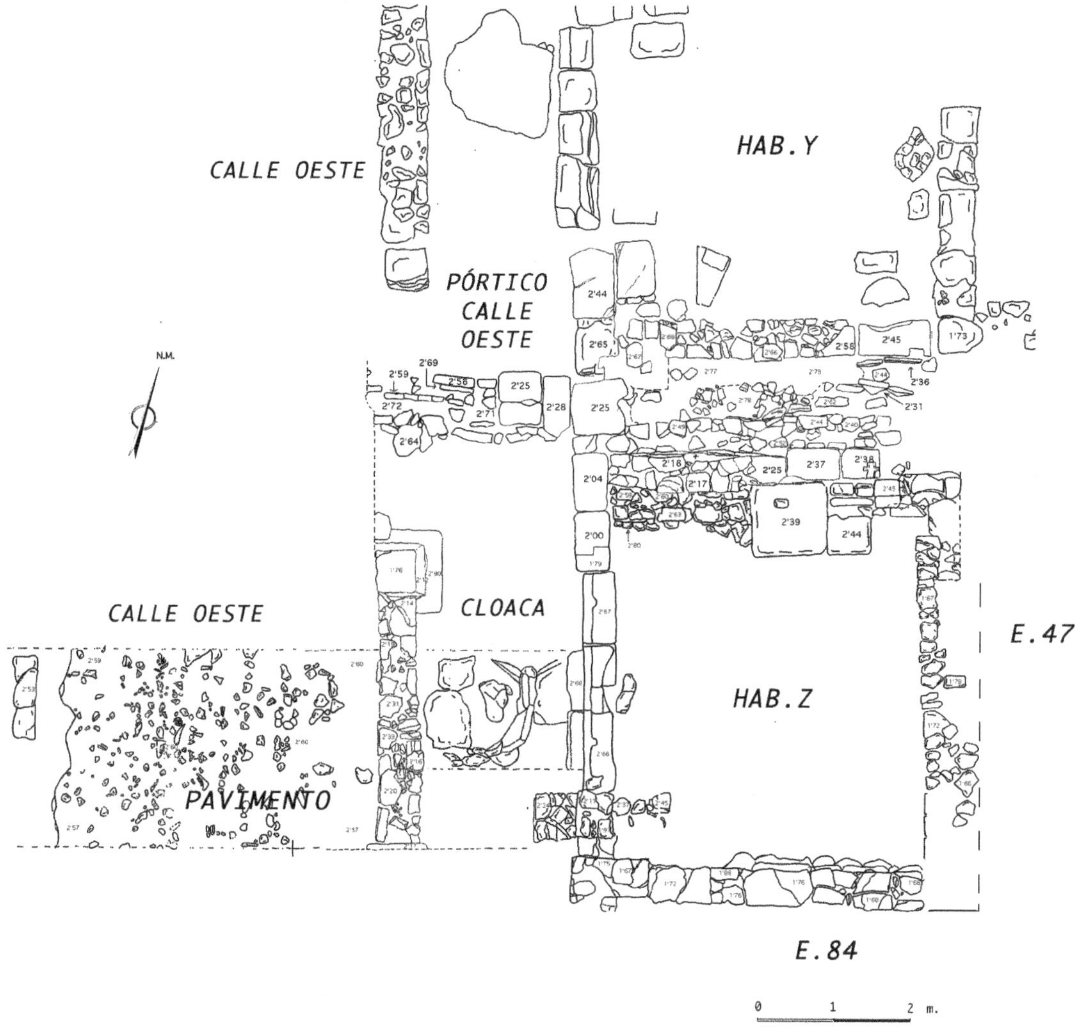

Fig. 4.1 Room Z. and West Portico

shallow square pit, 0.45 x 0.45 m., full of white wood ashes. At the southeast corner of the block is a smaller rectangular flat stone, 0.54 x 0.48 m., at depth 2.41. The large block and the smaller stones east of it are lying flat on the latest floor of the room at depth 2.64. Small leveling stones may be seen around the edges of the large block. The purpose of the block is uncertain. It may have been the base for a counter or workbench at the northeast entrance to the room.

The east wall of the room E-36 is 3.60 m. long. It buts up against the south wall of the room and is not joined to it. The wall is not perpendicular to the south wall, but lies at an angle of 85° to that wall. The fact that it rests on the second or early Imperial floor of the room indicates that when it was built a larger Republican room was divided in two. Room Z is, thus, the western half of the larger complex. Wall E-36 was broken approximately 1.00 south from the northeast corner of the room by a trench of the earlier excavators. The wall is made up of irregular courses of ashlar and trapezoidal blocks along with smaller irregularly shaped stones, amphora

fragments, and roof tiles, all bonded with clay. The excavator suggests that the upper two courses of larger blocks were added to the wall in an early third century reconstruction of the room. At its south end the wall was damaged by a hole for an almond tree. The bottom of the wall is at depth 2.65, the top at depth 2.10-2.20.

The south wall E-84 of Room Z is made up of four lower courses of ashlar blocks of varying sizes and above them four courses of irregularly shaped stones also varying in size, all bonded with clay. The wall has been exposed for a distance of 4.50 m. east from the southwest corner of the room, but almost certainly it continues eastward along the south side of the larger Republican complex. The excavator believes that the four upper courses of the wall were added as part of the third century reconstruction of the room. The bottom of the wall including leveling stones is at depth 2.91, the top at depth 1.66.

The main feature of the west wall of Room Z (E-47) is the expansive entrance, 2.86 m. wide. The section north of the entrance is 1.52 m. long and is made up of four courses of finely-cut large ashlar blocks bonded with clay. The footing to this section is at depth 2.80, the top of the wall at depth 1.52. The section south of the entrance is 0.85 m. long and is made up of small and largish stones in no order bonded by clay. This section of the wall buts up against the south wall of the room and is not joined to it. The footing to this section is at depth 3.24, its top at depth 1.90. At the south end of the entrance a short wall, 0.70 m. long, projects eastward into the room. The wall is made up of three courses of ashlar blocks, 0.25 m. wide. The footing for the wall is at depth 2.90, its top at depth 2.25. The purpose of this short wall is unclear. It does provide for a kind of alcove between it and the south wall of the room.

All of the stone walls of the room served as sills for mud brick sections above them. It is probable that the south wall was constructed first, followed in order by the west wall and then by the north wall. The east wall came later. The entrance threshold is made up of three large flat blocks, 0.96, 0.78, and 1.14 m. long x 0.60 m. wide, at depth 2.64. Running the length of the threshold at its center is a channel, 0.10 wide x 0.05 m. deep, for holding in place the wooden door or closure to the room. At the center of the threshold where the central stone meets the south stone a built drain, 0.42 long x 0.32 wide x 0.50 m. deep, passes through the footing of the wall under the threshold blocks. Inside the room the drain is framed with fragments of *opus signinum* pavement, outside the room with thin marés slabs. The drain empties into a round catch basin or cistern, 1.50 m. in diameter, in the porch or portico in front of Room Z. Fragments of the broken cover stone of the basin were found in the basin. Pottery from the catch basin indicates that it was dug in the late first century B.C. and went out of use during the reign of the Emperor Tiberius.

The earliest floor or pavement in Room Z is at depth 3.05. A small patch of the pavement has been preserved at the northwest corner of the room. It consists of small flat marés stones set in a bedding of clay. Fill beneath the pavement dates it to the end of the first quarter of the first century B.C. Set into this floor were six Italic amphorae (Dressel 1B), four of which were aligned parallel to the entrance to the room. At some point later in the first century B.C. a fill, 0.36 m. deep, was put down over this early floor. The fill was packed with amphora fragments and fragments of black glaze, fine-wall, hand-made Talayotic, and coarse wares along with animal and bird bones, suggesting that it came from a dump site. Three fragments of *terra sigillata precox* pottery may date the fill to ca. 50-40 B.C. Over this fill a second floor was laid at depth ca. 2.68. A small patch of this pavement made up of a sand and lime mixture, 0.10-0.15 thick, is preserved east of the north end of the doorway. This second floor dates, according to the excavator, to the time of a general renovation of the room

in the early first century A.D. It served as the floor of the room into the third century when the room collapsed.[4]

Over the latest floor was a layer of destruction debris, 0.30 deep, burnt mud brick mainly along the north side of the room, broken roof tiles, and pottery fragments. Only a few metal objects or other artifacts were found on the floor. Pottery in the fill was amphora fragments, *sigillata Africana* A and C wares, North African common wares, and Roman common pottery, all datable to the second half of the third century. Over the destruction rubble was a mass of roof tiles from the collapsed roof of the room. Directly over the roof tiles at the center of the room was a mound of soft white clay from depths 1.85 to 2.38. The clay may have come from the collapse of the mud brick walls of the room. Finally above the white clay was red earth into which many large and small building blocks had fallen in a line from southeast to northwest.

4.4 West Street and Portico

The excavators in 1997 opened a trench, 7.50 east to west x 2.50 m. south to north along the south side of Squares G-22 and G-23 west from the entrance to Room Z. The objective was to examine the West street and determine its width. At a distance of 7.00 m. west from the entrance to the room a narrow wall running south to north was found marking the west side of the street. At a distance of 2.00 m. from the entrance to the room is another wider wall, part of a porch or portico in front of Room Z. The latest surface of the West street is of small marés stones set in clay at depth 2.57. The street at this point is 4.50 m. wide.[5] (Fig. 4.1)

In 1998 two additional soundings were excavated in the west porch or portico, one directly in front of the entrance to Room Z at the east end of the 1997 sounding, the other at the north end of the entrance. In the south sounding the excavators found the round catch basin or cistern, 1.50 m. in diameter, with its broken cover stone. Along the south side of the sounding they were able to document a stratigraphic sequence from the end of the first quarter of the first century B.C. to the last half of the third century A.D. Data from the sounding confirmed earlier findings that Roman settlement at Pollentia began toward the end of the first quarter of the first century B.C. Stratigraphic evidence in both soundings indicates that the earliest pavement in the porch or portico in front of Room Z may be dated to the early first century A.D.[6] The pavement surface at depth 2.85 at the entrance to the

---

[4] Doenges in 1995 identified a beaten earth surface or floor of compact gray to yellow clay at depth 2.75-2.85, perhaps the top of the deep fill. The latest floor or surface along the north side of the room on which the structure collapsed was found to be at depth 2.64.

[5] Orfila 2000: 104-121.

[6] Pottery fragments in the Republican fill included 91 Republican amphora (mainly Dressel 1a and 1c), 10 Iberian, 5 black glaze A and B, 7 Italian kitchen ware, and one Dressel 3 lamp.

S N

4998

2 —

4997=5424=5383

5451=5351 5334=5335=5336=5387 → 5401

5342

5397 5335

5405 5389 5386 → 5351

3 — 5403 5351 5524 5474 5474=5494
5494

5411 5533

5440 5444 5428 5353 5353 5548 5542 5496
5561 5570
5571 → 5565

5344

5502 → 5495 5520
(Revoco interno
de las paredes
5523 5503 del pozo)

4 — 5549

5538

5539

5538

5569

5 — 5581

5582

5582 5657
UME 3

5655

5656 5656
5667 5694

5698 5699

6 — 5705 5698
5703

5706

7 — 5713

5717
(Terreno Natural)

Sección S-N
Pórtico Calle W
Ínsula de Tabernas al W del Foro

Losas de la cubierta del Pozo Negro
fracturadas y hundidas

Recorte del Pozo (5501)

0 0'5 1 m

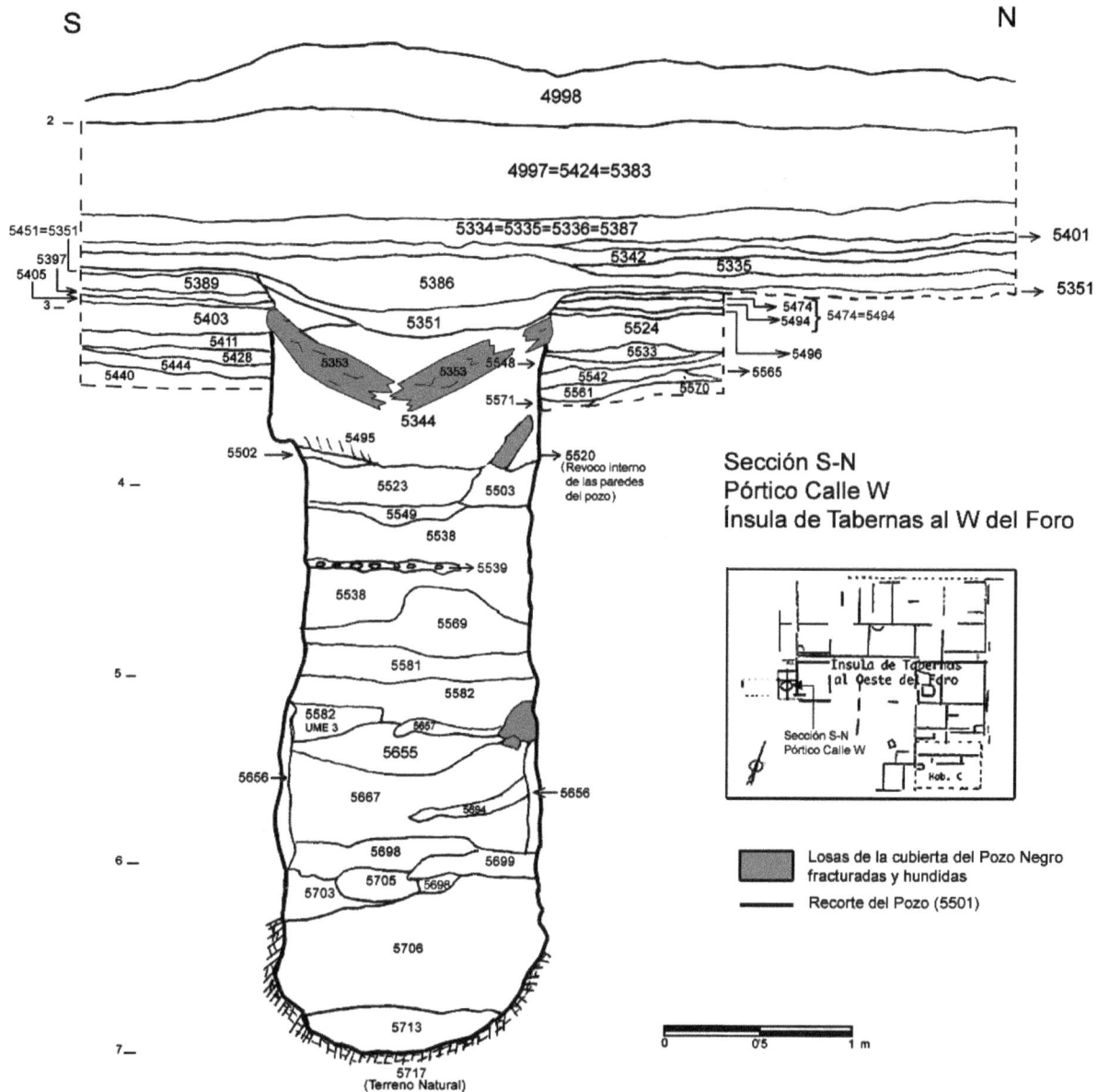

Fig. 4.2 Cistern in the West Portico.

room consisted of small marés stones set in clay. North of the entrance the surface was of beaten earth only. Over the earliest pavement was a deep fill of *blanquet*[7] and marés stones from depths 2.85 to 2.70. Over this fill was a second higher pavement of beaten earth at depth 2.65. Pottery evidence from the *blanquet* fill dates this second pavement to the late first century or early second century A.D. In the north sounding a rectangular base, 1.00 x 0.70 m., for a pilaster at the north end of the low wall in front of Room Z was isolated. On the base only one drum of the pilaster, 0.60 x 0.50 x 0.30 m., remains in place. The base rests on the Augustan pavement,

evidence that the porch or portico in front of Room Z was constructed no earlier than the turn of the millennium.[8]

---

[7] "*Blanquet*" is earth with a high concentration of lime which the excavator believes the Romans used to level areas of the forum before construction.

[8] The excavator proposes that the pilaster and those in front of Room Y belong to a portico along the west side of the *taberna insula* corresponding to the colonnaded portico on its east side. But the pilasters with a low wall between them are centered on the doorways to Rooms Y and Z. There is no wall between pilasters 2 and 3, and there is no evidence of pilasters or a wall in front of Room V. It may, therefore, be the case that by the beginning of the third century the pilasters and low walls in front of Rooms Y and Z belonged to a roofed porch projecting into the street or a low protective screen in front of the wide entrances to the rooms.

Over the early second century pavement of the portico was another fill, a very compact mixture of red earth and clay, in the area north of the entrance to Room Z at depths 2.62-2.57. The excavator regards this fill as preparation for a pavement at a still higher level. In this fill was an As of Marcus Aurelius dated to 179-180 A.D. as well as fragments of *sigillata Africana* A and C. This evidence would date the fill to the late second or early third century A.D. When the fill was put down, the height of the third pilaster was raised with the addition of two blocks, and a low wall was constructed between the pilasters in front of Room Z. To this period also belongs a square platform, 1.00 x 1.00 m., projecting into the passageway of the porch or portico at the south end of the entrance to Room Z. The excavator proposes that the platform served as a counter for display of goods in front of the shop. In the destruction fill over the latest pavement of the passageway at the entrance to the room were bits of carbonized wood from the door to the room, many iron nails, part of a bronze attachment, and an iron knife, debris from the fire which destroyed the shop.

The cistern in the portico at the entrance to Room Z was fully excavated during successive campaigns in 2000 and 2001. It was found to be 4.00 m. deep. (Fig. 4.2) Its cover stone was roughly at the level of the Augustan pavement of the portico. Ceramic evidence from the fill suggests that it was dug no earlier than 10 B.C. and ceased to be used during the rule of Tiberius ca. 30 A.D. Its closure may be associated with the renovations to Room Z in the early first century.

In extending northward the north sounding during the campaign of 1999, the excavators came upon three cover stones of a built drain running across the portico along the line of the walkway between Rooms Y and Z. The drain was fully excavated in 2000 and 2001. (Fig. 4.3) The north and south sides of the drain are made of thin marés slabs set vertically along the channel. Pottery from fill over the drain and in the channel was a mixture dating from the end of the first century to the beginning of the third century but with the latest pottery at the lowest levels and the earliest in the upper levels, a situation which suggests that the drain had been excavated as part of a trench dug in the 1920s or 1930s which was then refilled. Pottery, however, from contexts not touched by the earlier excavators indicates that the drain was constructed at some point in the first century A.D. and was remodeled with the channel at a higher level in the middle of the second century.

Discovery of the portico drain prompted further investigation of the walkway between Rooms Y and Z. As early as 1997 it was recognized that the walkway served not only as a passage or alley between the rooms but also as a runway or drain for water from the roofs of the structures on either side. (Fig. 4.1) The hard-packed bottom of the drain or the surface of the walkway is at depths 2.40 to 2.49. It is marked by the top of a low wall constructed along the north wall of Room Z and serving

as a kind of south border to the walkway. The drain exited into the portico of the west street by way of a large marés block at the façade of Rooms Y and Z. The block was hollowed out to form a low arch through which water passed into the portico. Beneath this drain was an earlier drain formed on its south side by the low wall abutting Room Z and on its north side by a wall of small stones packed in mortar. (Fig. 4.4) Materials from the north wall and from the foundation of the built south wall date the construction of the lower drain to early in the first half of the first century A.D. Pottery evidence suggests that the drain was in use throughout the first century. The date of the later drain is uncertain but may be placed in the second century. Sadly the trench of the earlier excavators which also cut through the portico removed many of the construction features of the upper drain, but it exposed the lower drain as it did the portico drain. The earlier excavators seem to have cleaned out the channel of the lower drain, and in refilling the trench, they packed the channel with loose stones. The connection between the two walkway drains and those in the portico is uncertain. The portico drains veer off in a west-northwesterly direction from the line of the walkway drains. The juncture between the two systems has yet to be investigated.

Fig. 4.3 View of the Portico drain.

Fig. 4.4 View of the lower walkway drain.

4.5 Room A

Room A is located at the southeast corner of the *taberna insula* facing the open area of the forum.[9] It occupies parts of Squares F-17 and F-18 on the grid plan of the forum. (Fig. 4.5) The room was excavated during the 1980s to the level of the latest floor at depth 2.02. In the late third century it was bound on the north by wall E-2, on the west by wall E-13, on the south by wall E-10, and on the east by wall E-6. The entrance to the room in the third century was 2.60 m. wide. The doorway threshold made up of three large flat blocks has a channel, 0.15 wide x 0.05 m. deep, for holding the wooden door or closure to the room. At the southeast corner of the room was a square platform or counter, 1.00 x 1.00 m. In the third century the room measured 4.50 west to east x 4.00 m. north to south.

It was decided in 1996 to excavate Room A in depth with the objective of recovering the history of the shops along the west side of the forum. The earliest floor of the room, it was learned, was of small flat marés stones set in clay at depths 2.45-2.51. Data from the fill over the floor

---

[9] Orfila, Arribas, and Cau 1999: 106 and 110 and Orfila 2000: 77-81.

dates the pavement to the first half of the first century B.C. On this surface the Republican south wall of the room E-31 was constructed. Only two courses of this wall, 3.00 m. long, remain in place immediately north of the third century south wall of the room. Thus the room in the Republican period was slightly smaller than it was in the third century, measuring, 4.50 x 3.56 m.

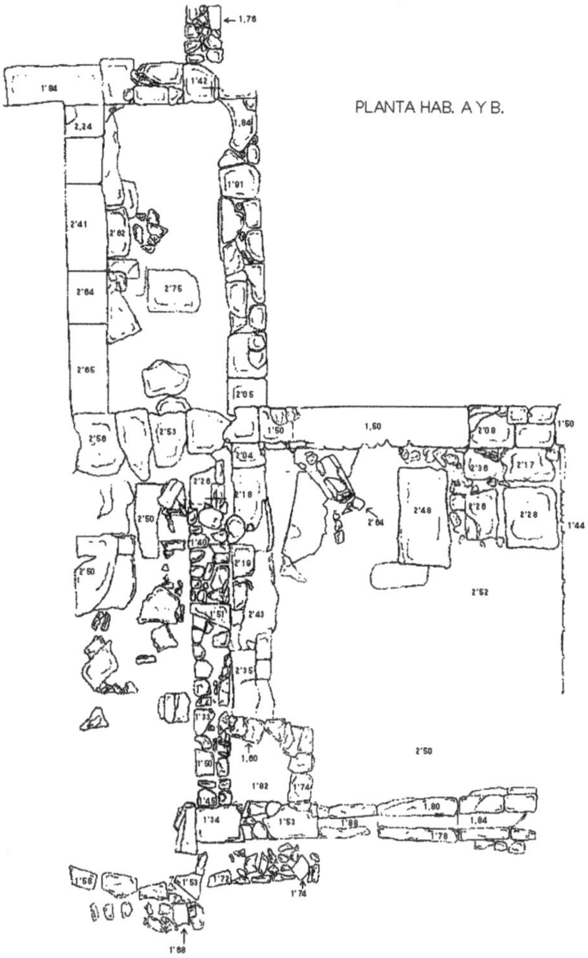

Fig. 4.5 Rooms A and B

Over the Republican floor of the room a deep fill was put down at some point still in the first century B.C. Through this fill and penetrating the Republican floor an oval catch basin, 2.20 x 1.60 m., was dug at the southwest corner of the room. (Fig. 4.6) Two large flat blocks covered the catch basin, one of which had a hole cut through it. Over the cover stones was more fill, earth with many small stones. In this fill and resting on the west wall of the room was a drain made of flat marés stones running from the wall to the hole in the cover of the basin. Fragments of *terra sigillata classica* from the opening to the basin date the basin to the early first century A.D. The excavators did not identify a surface or floor at the level of the top or bottom of the cover stones. At some point in the third century A.D. there occurred a major reconstruction of Room A. A new beaten earth floor was put down at depth 2.02. The height of the north wall was raised with the addition of three courses of what seem to be large reused blocks from other buildings. This upper section of the wall is wider than the Republican wall beneath it. Similarly the west wall of the room was raised. There may have been at this point a doorway from Room A into Room F through the west wall at the northwest corner of the room. A new south wall E-10 six to seven courses high was constructed south of the Republican wall, enlarging the area of the room. The excavators believe that the east wall of the room with its doorway belongs as well to the third century reconstruction of the room.

Fig. 4.6 Covered oval catch basin in Room A

4.6 Room B

Room B is a corridor or passageway, 1.50 m. wide, between Rooms A and F to the north and Room C to the south.[10] (Fig. 4.5) The room was excavated by Isasi in the 1920s and refilled with a mixture of earth and large building stones. In 1996 it was decided to remove the Isasi fill in order to study the area in depth. That step exposed the earliest phase of the room for examination.

---

[10] Orfila, Arribas, and Cau 1999: 106-107 and Orfila 2000: 83-89.

The room is bound on the north by walls E-19 and E-31 and on the south by walls E-72 and E-117. In its early phases the room was divided in two by wall E-70 running north to south along the line of the west wall of Room A. Until the third century the passageway remained open at its east and west ends. In the third century wall E-73 was constructed between Rooms F and C closing Room B on the west.

All of the walls of Room B were built on the earliest surface or pavement of the corridor. Indeed, except for walls E-19 and E-72 in the west half of the room only large irregularly shaped footing stones for the walls remain in place. Wall E-19 between Rooms B and F is made up of four courses of small blocks bonded by clay. Wall E-72 is well constructed with large regularly shaped marés blocks. It supports the *opus signinum* pavement of Room C along its north side.

The earliest surface or pavement in Room B at depth 2.55 is of small marés stones set in clay. Data from the *blanquet* fill beneath this floor date it to the first half of the first century B.C. It is on this surface that the footings for all of the walls of the room rest.

At the southwest corner of Room A where the third century walls of that room have been broken a small patch of fill, 0.40 m,[2] remained undisturbed by the earlier excavators. This patch provides a stratigraphic sequence for changes in Room B from the late Republic to the third century A.D. Over the Republican surface of the room is a *blanquet* fill. It served as a base for a marés pavement at depth 2.22 dating perhaps to the early first century A.D. The excavator proposes that at this stage the dividing wall E-70 was removed and Room B became a passageway between Room C and the shops to the north.[11] Over the second pavement was a thin layer of ashes, indicating that the room suffered damage by fire. Over the ashes is more fill to the level of use in the third century at depth 2.02. In that century the east half of Room B was narrowed by the construction of the new south wall E-10 of Room A, and the room was closed at its west end by the construction of wall E-73 and perhaps by a wall at its east end.

At a late date walls E-73 and E-19 at the northwest corner of Room B were damaged by the digging of a well. The exact date of the well remains uncertain as it has not been excavated.

---

[11] It is not certain that the wall was destroyed at this point in time. The undisturbed stratigraphic patch does not extend over the line of wall E-70. It is possible that the changes in Room B indicated in the stratigraphic profile occurred only in the eastern half of the room. In the Republican and early Imperial periods Room B may have served to frame wooden staircases to the upper floors of Rooms A and F. By the third century it became a dead end alley.

4.7 Sounding west of the Capitolium

In 1999 and 2000 a sounding, 7.20 x 2.50 m., was excavated between the entrance to Room O and the west side of the Capitolium podium between the third and fourth columns of the west colonnade in Squares H-15, 16, and 17. The objective was to study the relationship between the shops on the west side of the forum and the temple. The portico on the west side of the forum is 2.70 m. wide, the passage or street between the portico and the Capitolium 5.00 m. wide.

The excavators learned that the lowest stratum over bed rock in the sounding is a layer of *blanquet*, 0.15 m. deep. This stratum of *blanquet* in the passageway slopes gradually downward from east to west from depth 2.40 to depth 2.64. The *blanquet* layer, it is proposed, was put down as a leveling course in preparation for the construction of the Capitolium. Over the *blanquet* is a stratum of red clay mixed with *blanquet*, 0.30 m. deep, also sloping downward from east to west at depths 2.30 to 2.47 m. The excavator identifies this red clay stratum as the pavement of the forum in the first century B.C. It was on this surface that the west portico was constructed. Unfortunately it was not possible to determine its relation to the Capitolium because a trench had been excavated in 1988 along the west face of the only section of the west wall of the temple podium still standing.

In the passageway between the temple podium and the colonnade there were four holes, 0.20 to 0.25 m. in diameter, dug into the Republican pavement in a line east to west. The excavator suggests that they may have held posts to support an awning stretching over the street between the Capitolium and the colonnade.

In studying the footing of the fourth column of the west portico, the excavators learned that it was set in a trench, 1.40 x 1.40 m., dug into the *blanquet* leveling stratum to bed rock. The footing stone itself is a large square marés block, 0.85 x 0.85 x 0.57 m. high. On its upper surface is a circular marking, 0.64 m. in diameter, where the column base once stood. To insure stability of the footing, the foundation trench was packed with a mixture of red clay and small stones. Pottery in the fill dates the footing stone to the first half of the first century B.C., in particular, a fragment of an Ebusitan amphora, form PE18.

Over the Republican pavement in the sounding was a fill of earth and small marés stones and above it a compact layer of earth and lime at depth 2.24 which the excavator identifies as a second pavement of the portico and passageway. Pottery from both strata date this second pavement to the early second century A.D.

Finally at the beginning of the third century two layers of earth at depths 2.23-2.18 were put down over the second century pavement in order to level the portico and street. On this fill walls were constructed between the columns

of the portico converting it into a long narrow enclosed space in front of the shops. Over the fill at the entrance to Room O there were a few scattered patches of beaten clay pavement at depth 2.15. Directly in front of the doorway to Room O a low narrow stone bench, one flat slab high, was placed perhaps to display goods from the shop. The bench like the walls rests on the third century fill. It was on the third century surface or pavement that the portico collapsed during the second half of the century.

4.8 Late Fortification System

One meter north from the northwest corner of the Capitolium a massive platform or tower, 5.00 north to south x 4.80 west to east x 1.50 m. high, was exposed during the excavations of the 1980s. The platform is solidly built with reused building blocks, including half column drums and cornice pieces probably taken from nearby structures, all held together with crumbly mortar. The platform is joined to the Capitolium podium by a low pile of material, broken ashlar blocks and small stones, in a fill of *blanquet*.

Running west from the platform 3.20 m. south from the northwest corner of the tower is a well-constructed wall, one of the finest preserved in Pollentia. The wall which has been exposed for a distance of 10.00 m. west from the tower is made up of three courses of reused marés building blocks, some of them cushioned, resting on a wide footing set on bed rock. The wall is bonded with coarse mortar, and the courses are leveled with pottery or roof tile fragments.

In examining the wall in 1999 and 2000, the excavator concluded that it was the north face of a massive fortification wall along the north side of the Capitolium and the *taberna insula*.[12] Indeed, the north wall of the Capitolium podium and the north walls of the *insula*, it is proposed, provided the south face of the defensive wall. Only at the north end of the portico along the west side of the Forum are there four stones of the south face of the wall still in place. No evidence of the south face of the wall has been found at the north end of the passageway between the portico and the Capitolium. Fill between the north and south faces of the wall consists of many large and small building blocks taken from nearby structures packed in a mixture of gravel, earth, and sandy mortar. In some places it appears that large reused blocks lying flat served as a kind of bed for the earth and rubble fill above. The excavator estimates that the defensive wall was 4.46 m. wide.

East of the platform or tower only one or two blocks from the north face of the defensive wall remain in place. In the early 1990s excavators used a bulldozer to remove what at the time was thought to be refill of an early

---

[12] Orfila, Arribas, and Cau 1999: 113-116 and Orfila 2000: 123-130.

excavation trench. It now seems that the material carted away belonged to the late fortification wall.

The date of the fortification system north of the Capitolium is uncertain. In the early 1990s a third century funerary inscription was identified in the north face of the defensive wall. In the foundation trench of the wall were a few fragments of *sigillata Africana* D pottery as well as a single sherd of what may be *fabrica Moscovita* ware, Hayes 91, for which the excavator suggests a date in the fifth century or later. Latest pottery in the robber trench over the wall was Islamic wares. A date for the fortification system in the fifth or sixth century raises questions as to why such a massive wall was built in that period and what was left of Pollentia to merit protecting. The only remains found in the area of the forum and the *taberna insula* dating to the period after the destructive fire of the late third century are two sizable fragments of *opus signinum* pavement, one at depth 1.82 in Square H-22 and the other in Square J-18, a solidly built corner of a late structure at depth 1.73 in Square I-22, a possible late room south of the Capitolium, and some two hundred graves in a semi-circle south, east, and north of the Capitolium. One of the graves was dug into the northwest corner of the platform or tower of the fortification system. It is also possible that Room R in the *taberna insula* survived or was restored after the fire. Thus far the only securely datable finds from the forum excavations between the third century and the Islamic period are a few fragments of *terra sigillata Africana* D pottery and even fewer coins from the fourth century.[13] It is possible that the late fortification wall was the result of an impulse immediately after the third century fire to protect the Capitolium which was still standing. But that impulse was soon abandoned in favor of a plan to fortify the residential area at Sa Portella to which the population of the city retreated and which had not been affected by the great fire. The history of the area north of the Capitolium and the taberna insula awaits further investigation.

4.9 Forum Pavements and Late South Room

In the summers of 2000 and 2001 a trench, 9.00 west to east x 2.60 m. south to north, was excavated between Room C and the altar or *aedicula* at the southwest corner of the Capitolium. The objective of the excavation was to examine further the pavement levels of the Forum and to study a Late Roman room which had been partially excavated in the 1980's between the altar and Room C. (Fig. 4.7)

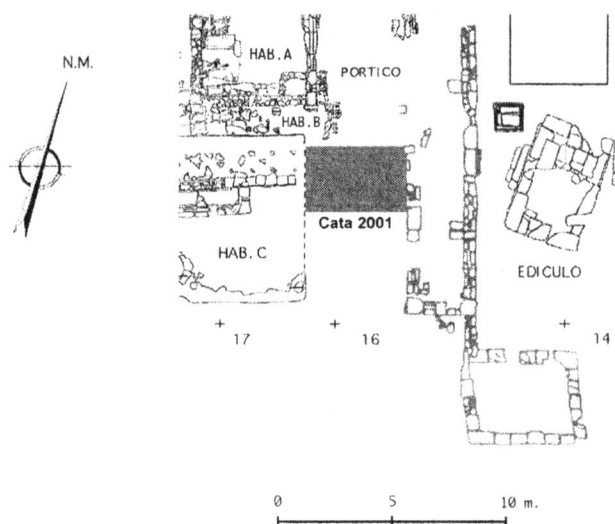

Fig.4.7 Location of the sounding between Room C and the Altar

The earliest pavement of the Forum identified in the sounding between the Late South Room and the altar was of beaten earth at depth 2.40. Pottery in the fill seems to date the pavement to the beginning of the first century A. D.

Between the altar and the east wall of the Late South Room a second higher beaten earth pavement was identified at depth 2.22. The excavators date this pavement to the end of the first century or beginning of the second century on the basis of a fragment of *Terra Sigillata Africana* A and a fragment of North African kitchen ware found in the pavement fill. This pavement like the earlier one clearly ran under the altar and the Late South Room.

Over the second pavement was a fill or surface consisting of earth and small fragmented marés stones at depth 2.12. Pottery in the fill dates it to the second century only a few years after the second pavement. It is on this surface that the altar or *aedicula* seems to rest. If so, the altar is to be dated to the second century and is not the oldest structure in the Pollentia Forum as was thought previously. The excavator continues to investigate the date of the altar.

Evidence for third century or later occupation is completely lacking in the area between the Late South Room and the altar. The reason may be that it was removed during the excavations of the early 1980s. But in the area west of the Late South Room a thin fill of compact earth, possibly a pavement, 0.06 to 0.12 m. deep, over the second century surface may date to the third or fourth century. The fill remains partially unexcavated, but two fragments of *Terra Sigillata Africana* D ware from it suggests a date in the late third or fourth century.

---

[13] Only twelve coins from the first half of the fourth century and four coins from the second half of the century ending with an *Aes* of Theodosius I (383-387 A.D.) have been found in the Forum excavations. All but two of these coins were associated with graves in the Forum necropolis. No coins from the fifth to the high Medieval period have as yet been found. See Mattingly below, pp. 60-61. On the evidence for a date in the fifth or sixth century for the fortification system see Orfila, Arribas, and Cau 1999: 115-116.

It is on this late compact fill that the west and east walls of the Late South Room rest. The Late South Room is part of a complex of three rooms constructed perhaps in the fourth century along the line of the west portico east of the portico itself. When the rooms were laid out, the street west of the Capitolium had ceased to function. The Late South Room is 2.00 wide west to east x perhaps 4.00 m. long north to south. The two walls are made up of reused blocks, 0.50 to 0.55 tall x 0.40 m. wide, with their short sides set directly on the surface of the fill. In the west wall there is a doorway, 1.04 m. wide, with a slightly raised threshold located at the south side of the trench.

The earliest floor of the Late South Room at depth 1.81 was of beaten earth. On it was a built hearth, 0.40 x 0.38 m., situated 0.20 m. east from the west wall of the room. The hearth was edged with two stones, and an amphora fragment served as a heat refractor at its center. It was found filled with ashes and bits of carbon. On the floor of the room near the hearth were scraps of lead, suggesting that lead was being worked.

At depth 1.75 there was a second floor of compact gray clay in the Late South Room. Above it was a third floor of very compact white clay at depth 1.69. On this pavement rests a buttress, 0.65 x 0.60 x 0.40 m., built against the east wall of the room. The buttress is made up of two marés blocks standing vertically and bonded with earth. In this same phase the doorway into the room was walled shut with a large reused building stone. During the period in which the Late South Room was in use the area west of the room seems to have served as a dumping ground for broken pottery and animal bones. After the room ceased to be occupied, a fill, 0.20 m. deep, of earth and small stones accumulated over it to depth 1.60. This fill was disturbed in the excavations of the 1980s so that it was not possible to determine whether it was purposely deposited to level the area of the Forum or simply accumulated over time.

Excavation in the area of the Forum continues each summer under the direction of Dra. Orfila. Preliminary reports on the work are submitted annually to the *Consell Insular de Mallorca.*

Chapter 5

POLLENTIA: HISTORY AND COINAGE

Harold B. Mattingly

Since the early 1970's excavators at Pollentia have had two main aims.[1] One was to determine the line of the west and north walls of the town. The west wall survived, and the north presumably coincided with the line of Alcudia's mediaeval wall. The other aim was to reveal and explore the central area of the town – its shops, houses, public buildings, temples, and shrines. The walled area turned out to be very limited: it enclosed the residential Sa Portella district and not much more.[2] A date for its construction not much later than the reign of Probus seems likely. That reign saw busy fortification in mainland Spain and Gaul. Tarraco was sacked by the Franks c. A.D. 262, and other towns were badly affected about the same time. A general overhaul of defenses seems to have ensued.[3] In north Gaul, even more exposed to barbarian raids, towns like Beauvais, Senlis, Soissons, and Amiens built walls in or after the 270's, enclosing much reduced urban areas from 6.5 to 12 hectares. Some of these were built over ruined buildings and constructed out of salvaged material.[4]

The Forum area and the House of Polymnia were left well outside the walls. Depopulation had already set in, and they were probably now abandoned. In the Ca'n Reinés area the continuous coin record breaks off with three reform coins of Tacitus and Probus and never recovers. Only nine bronze coins cover the period from A. D. 284 to 341.[5] From some point in the fourth century the area began to be used for burials, and most of the later coins and pottery are associated with tombs.[6] The House of Polymnia was destroyed before the abandonment of the Forum and the retreat of the disheartened population to the Sa Portella site. The date is fixed by a hoard of 33 bronze coins and an antoninianus of Gallienus from 253/4. The latest bronze coins are three sestertii of the Philips and Trebonianus Gallus in fine condition. No later coins were found in this house.[7] Superficially a date in the 250's would seem required, supported by another hoard from Ca'n Reinés. That hoard was also associated with local destruction evidence and came down to a sestertius of Valerian from A.D, 253/4. But sestertius hoards with this composition must be treated with caution. The sestertii of Decius, Gallus, and Valerian in the Ca'n Reinés hoard show some wear. Moreover there is a curious break in the provision of new coinage at Pollentia. In the 1957-69 list there is a gap between the sestertii of Valerian and Salonina and the antoninianus of Gallienus' fifth issue of c. A.D. 265/6.[8] The excavators at Conimbriga found a very similar break in provision of currency at this time.[9] We should probably date the two Pollentia hoards in the early 260's or even later. By c. A.D. 265 normal circulation was restored and Gallienus' coinage appears in significant numbers. Another coin of his fifth issue was found at nearby Bocchoris c. 1971, and

---

[1] I must thank Professors Daniel Woods, Miguel Tarradell, Antonio Arribas, and Norman Doenges for their help, encouragement, and patience over many years. With the last two I have had the advantage of close discussions of the problems on and off the site. [This article was written for inclusion in a planned vol. 5 of the Pollentia series published by the Bryant Foundation. That volume never materialized. The article appears here with permission of the author.]

[2] See M. Tarradell, A. Arribas, and G. Rosselló Bordoy, *Historia de Alcudia I* (1978) 281-291.

[3] On Tarraco see Eutropius 9.9.2; Victor, *Caesars* 35.3; Orosius 7.22.8; Eusebius-Jerome p. 221 Helm; G. Alföldy, *RE* Suppl. XV (1978), col. 598 ff. Despite Eusebius' precise date (A.D. 264) modern scholars put the raid a little earlier. See Alföldi and S. J. Keay, *Roman Spain* (1988) 177. Emporiai seems to have been virtually abandoned from the 260's perhaps because of these troubles. See J. Aquileu, J. M. Nolla, and E. Sanmartí, *MDAI* (Madrid) 27 (1986) 225-234. But J. Nieto, *Rev. Etud. Ligur.* 47 (1981) 34-51, has argued that Emporiai foundered *before* the barbarian raids. For the effect on other Spanish towns see J. Sanchez Real, *Bolletin Arq.* 51 (1951) 129 ff. and 57 (1957) 6 ff. Some building and rebuilding of walls in Spain like the Proban activity in Gaul seems to have been delayed till Diocletian. See Keay, pp. 178-81.

[4] See Stephen Johnston, *Britannia* 4 (1973) 210-213; R. Namoune and A. Muller, *Rev. du Nord* 67 (1985) 183 ff. (Amiens wall dated by fine coin of Claudius II); A. Jacques, Marie Tuffrera-Libre, E. Delot, and D. Gricourt, *ibid.* pp. 75-99 (Arras, nine hectares circuit, one third of early imperial town) and 103 ff. (walls dated by a very fresh Tetricus I antoninianus).

[5] See the conspectus of excavation coins and contrast the record of the Sa Portella site in *Pollentia: Los materiales I* (1983) 275-277.

[6] This judgment can be easily tested from the conspectus and the site lists.

[7] The minim copy of Divo Claudio/Altar of A.D. 275-280 came from a well and should be discounted; likewise the dumpy Divo Claudio/Eagle copy from a 1977 trench. The few coins of the House of Constantine or the Valentinian period are surely strays like those from Ca'n Reinés. Over the ruins of the house and the buried hoard there was more than a meter of sterile soil. See *op. cit.* (note 2) 350.

[8] Gallic and British sestertius hoards ending with coins of c. A.D. 250 may have been buried in the late 260's. Not much mid-third century bronze was reaching those provinces for some reason. In Italy, Sardinia, and Africa the flow of new issues continued down to c. A.D. 260 at least. See T. V. Buttrey, *ANSMN* 18 (1972) 45-58. Pollentia looks a little closer to this pattern than I once thought. For *Victoria Aug. III* and *Pudicitia* see E. Besley and R. Bland, *The Cunetio Treasure* (1983) 25 ff. and 111, and for Oriens Aug. p. 117.

[9] See I. Pereira, J-P. Bost, and J. Kienard, *Fouilles de Conimbriga III: Les Monnaies* (1974).

there are three others in the 1957-69 record.[10] The burial of the hoards should be put down to fear caused by the barbarian inroads and the ensuing insecurity or else to trouble arising from the challenge of the Gallic Empire. Postumus had some following in eastern Spain though Claudius II restored central control after Postumus' death. Even in distant Emerita a monument of Gallienus was defaced after A.D. 261, and as late as the early 270's the names of Aurelian and Severina were erased at Tarraco.[11] All the shops at town center in Pollentia were destroyed in the 260's. Such events would have further encouraged the population to abandon the Forum and its neighborhood some fifteen years later. The contracted town continued to enjoy limited prosperity until the coming of the Vandals c. A.D. 425 led to the gradual abandonment of the whole site. [12]

On the early history of Roman Pollentia the recent excavations have confirmed my former conclusions from the coinage. The pattern of Roman and Iberian coinage on the site bears no relation to the Scipionic camps of 134-132 B.C. at Numantia. The material from early in the second century is consistently more worn.[13] The pattern is much closer to the camps of the Sertorian period. This conclusion is clearest with the denarii and quinarii which cluster in the period from c. 110 to 87 B.C.[14] The Romans took over the native settlement at Pollentia when they conquered the Balearics in 123 B.C. But they seem to have been in no hurry to exploit the site and were at first content to establish small *castella* here and at Palma. Pollentia seems to have developed as a town on the Roman model only in the 70's B.C. like Valentia. Its status as a Roman municipium like that of many comparable Spanish communities may prove to be due to Caesar.[15] From the Caesarian age certainly the town's

growth was steady, if unspectacular, and it appears to have recovered reasonably well from the troubles of the 260's and 270's. But the barbarians in the end had the last word.

Harold B. Mattingly

Cambridge

---

[10] For *Indulgentia Aug.* (Bocchoris), *Fortuna Redux, Securit. Perpet.*, and *Marti Propugnat* see *Cunetio* (1983) 116-118.

[11] See J. S. Drinkwater, *The Gallic Empire*, Hist. Einzelschr. 52 (1987) 116 ff., 120, 203 ff., and 211, on Postumus and Claudius. He suggests that Spain remained loyal to Aurelian (p. 123), but there was at least local discontent at Tarraco. See G. Alföldy, *RE* Suppl. XV, col. 599, and *AE* (1930) 150. J. L. Ramirez, J. J. Enriquez, and A. Lelazquez reported on the Gallienus monument at the Xth International Epigraphic Congress (Nîmes 1992).

[12] See the 1957-69 coin list in *op. cit.* (n. 5) 275-277 with comments on p. 248.

[13] See *op. cit.* (n. 5) 245 ff. For an excellent new study of the material from Nieblas III and the Scipionic camps see H. J. Huldebrandt, *MDAI* (Madrid) 20 (1970) 238-271.

[14] See the list p. 62 and in *op. cit.* (n. 5) 273, 282, and 285. Denarii of Flavus (C 207), Aburius (C 244 or 250), L. Flaminius Cilo (C 302), M. Herennius (C 308), and one quinarius of Cn. Egnatulei C. f. (C333) are on display at Lluc Monastery.

[15] R. C. Knapp, *Aspects of the Roman Experience in Iberia, 206-100 B.C.* (1977) 125-139, has argued that Valentia (founded c. 120 B.C.?) was closely comparable to Pollentia and Palma. After a humble start it first achieved real note as a town in the 70's. H. Galsterer, *Untersuchungen zum römischen Stadtwesen auf den Iberischen Halbinsel* (1971) 10 and 15,

claimed like Knapp that the Mallorcan towns were at first Latin colonies but were given charters as Roman *municipia* (*oppida civium Romanorum* in Pliny's phrase) in the Caesarian/Augustan period. On Caesar and Augustus in Spain see Galsterer, pp. 17-30, and M. Grant, *From Imperium to Auctoritas* (1946) 154-174. Grant does not deal specifically with Pollentia and Palma since neither struck coinage. For my earlier case see *op. cit.* (n. 5) 245 ff.

61

Conspectus of Excavation Coins, 1974 - 1990

1. Foreign coins of the Republican period (10)

Iberian As of Cese, 2nd/1st c. BC (CDF Room B).   [CDF = Camp d'en França]

Iberian As of Celsa, late 2nd c. BC (CDF '78).

Iberian semis of Celsa, c.100-60 BC (CR H/19).   [CR = Ca'n Reinés]

Heavy Iberian As of Emporiai, 2nd/1st c. BC (CR I/19).

4 Iberian Asses of Emporiai, c.60-50 BC (CDF B, N. Trench '78, Room 8: CR I/19-H/19).

Light Iberian As of Emporiai, c.60 BC (CR ?).

Latin As of Emporiai, c.40-30 BC (CR I/17).

2. Roman Republican Coinage (22)

7 anon. Republican Asses, c.200-145 BC (CDF Room 6,7 and '77, CR G/15, I/11(2), I/18).

As with symbol 'dog' (C 122), c.200 BC (CB).   [CB = Ca'n Bassé]

As with 'caps of the Dioscuri' (C 181), c.160 BC (CDF Room C).

2 Asses with 'anchor' before prow (C 194), c.160 BC (CDF Room 7: CR I/17).

As with 'ass' above prow (C 195), c.160 BC (CR Temple II in Forum).

Quadrans/sextans of c.150-40 BC? (CR Room M).

Sextans of c.150-40 BC? (CR F/10).

As of Safra (C 206/2), c.150 BC (CDF Room I).

As of C. Iuni C.f.(C 210), c.150 BC (CR I/15).

As of Q. Marc. Libo (C 215/2), c.150 BC (CB).

Sextans of Q. Marc. Libo (C 215/6), c.150 BC (CB).

As of C. Ter. Luc. (C 217/2), c.145 BC (CDF Room 2).

Core of plated denarius of Ti. Minuci C.f. Augurini (C 243/1) after 130 BC. (CB).

Plated(?) denarius of Lent. Marc. f. (C 329/1a) c.100 BC or later (CR J/17).

Plated(?) quinarius of Cn. Egnatulei C.f. (C 333) c.95 BC or later (CDF Room 2).

3. Foreign coinage of the Imperial period (4)

2 Latin duoviral Asses of Emporiai c.30 BC-AD 40 and c.AD 30 (CR Muralla, CDF Trench 9).

Latin As of Saguntum (*L. Ael.---Mag. aed. col.*) c.20 BC? (CR Room M).

Latin As of Caesaraugusta, AD 31/2 (CDF Room 8).

4. Roman Imperial Coinage: Augustus to Nero (41)

Sest. of Augustan moneyer: as *RIC* 1² 323, c.18-15 BC (CDF Room I).

6 Asses of Augustan moneyers: C. Plotius Rufus (15 BC), P. Lurius Agrippa (7 BC:2), M. Salvius Otho (7 BC:2), unknown (CDF Trench I, CR G/15 and FV, CDF Trench 10 and CR Cata 7, CR I/15-J/15).

5 1/2 Nemausus Asses: as *RIC* 1² 155-7, c.20-10 BC (CB(2), CDF Room I, CR Cata 7 and I/17, CR I/17).

Nemausus As: as *RIC* 1² 155-61, c. AD 10-14? (CR Trench 10).

As of Augustus (*RIC* 1² 471), AD 11/12 (CDF Room D).

As of Tiberius (*RIC* 1² 33-7), AD 15/6 (CR I/11).

3 Divus Augustus Pater Asses (*RIC* 1³ 80 f.: Altar), c. AD 23-30 (CB, CR Rooms 3 and 4).

2 Divus Augustus Pater Asses (*RIC* 1² 82: Eagle), c. AD 34-7 (CDF Room 6, CB).

As of Tiberius (*RIC* 1² 64-9), AD 36/7 (CR Trench II).

3 Asses of Gaius (Caligula) / *Vesta* (*RIC* 1² 38 and 54), AD 37/8 and 40/1 (FV, CDF Room B and Trench 10).

2 Asses of M. Agrippa (*RIC* 1² 58 (Gaius)), AD 37-41 (CDF Trench 12, CR Room M).

As of Claudius / rev. uncertain, AD 41-54 (CDF Trench 12).

6 Asses of Claudius / Minerva (as *RIC* 1³ 100,116), AD 41-54 (CDF '77 and'78, Trench 12 and Room 2, CR H/15 and I/15 - J/15).

3 Asses of Claudius / *Libertas Augusta* (as *RIC* 1² 97,113), AD 41-54 (CDF Trench 10 and '78, CR outside muralla).

2 Asses of Claudius / *Constantiae Augusti* (as *RIC* 1² 95 and 111), AD 41-54 (CR Trench 1 and I/15).

Quadrans of Claudius (*RIC* 1² 87), AD 41 (CDF Room B).

As of Nero / Victory flying lt. with shield (*RIC* 1² 312-6), AD 65-7 (CDF Room 1).

5 Roman Imperial Coinage: Vespasian to Commodus (103)

Denarius of Vespasian (plated?) / *Concordia Augusti* (BMC II 65) AD 72/3 or later (CR Trench II).

As of Vespasian / *Aequitas Augusti* (BMC II 702), AD 74-6 (CR Room M).

Sestertius of Titus / rev. illegible, AD 79-81 (CR H/17).

As of Domitian / rev uncertain, AD 84-96 (CDF Hoard).

As of Domitian / *Moneta Aug.* (as BMC II 298), AD 84-56 (FV)

Dup. of Domitian / *Moneta Aug.* (as *BMC* II 288), AD 84-96 (CR Trench VII).

Quadrans of Domitian / rhinocerus (as *BMC* II 496), AD 84-96 (CR Room M).

Dupondius of Domitian / *Saluti Augusti* (BMC II 291), AD 84 (CR J/17).

Semis of Domitian (*BMC* II 318: Apollo/raven), AD 85 (CDF Room 2).

3 Asses of Domitian / *Fortunae Augustae* (*BMC* II 401,448,468) AD 87, 90-1 and 92-4 (CR Room M).

As of Domitian / *Virtuti Aug.* (*BMC* II 452), AD 90/1 (CR Room M).

As of Nerva / *Aequitas Aug.* (*BMC* III 127), AD 97 (CDF Room B).

As of Nerva / *Libertas Publica* (as *BMC* III 131), AD 96-8 (CR H/15).

Denarius of Trajan (plated?) / *Virtus* or Mars?, AD 98-117 or later (CDF Room B).

As of Trajan / Victory lt. (*BMC* III 751-3), AD 101/2 (CR Room M).

Sest. of Trajan / Pax lt. (*BMC* III 745), AD 101/2 (CR Room M).

Dup./As of Trajan / Victory lt. crowns Trajan (as *BMC* III 899 (dup) or 941 (As)), AD 104-112 (CR H/17).

3 Asses of Hadrian / female fig. lt., AD 117-38 (CDF Room 9, CR C/16, and I/18).

4 sestertii of Hadrian / female fig. lt (stg. or std.), AD 117-38 (CR E/14, I/20, J/19 and Hoard).

As of Hadrian / *Salus Augusti* (as *BMC* III 1348), AD 117-38 (CDF Hoard).

As of Hadrian / *Annona Aug.*(as *BMC* III 1574), AD 117-38 (CDF Room 1).

Dup. of Hadrian / Mars rt. with trophy, AD 117-38 (CR G/10).

Dup. of Hadrian / *Pax* , AD 117-38 (CR I/17).

Dup. of Hadrian / *Annona Aug.* (as *BMC* III 1515), AD 117-38 (GR I/18).

Dup. of Hadrian / *Fort. Red.* (*BMC* III 1142), AD 118 (CDF Room Y).

2 sest. of Hadrian / *Fortuna Aug.* (as *BMC* III 1507), AD 119-38 (CR C/22 and Muralla)

Dup. of Hadrian / *Concordia?* (as *BMC* III 1582*?), AD 129-38 (CR Room D).

Sest./dup. of Hadrian / *Aegyptos* (as *BMC* III 1692-8(S) or 1699 ff.(D)), AD 134-6 (CR H/17).

As of L. Aelius Caesar / *Spes* (*BMC* III 1931-3), AD 137/8 (CR I/18).

2 dup. of Antoninus Pius / female fig.lt., AD 138-61 (CR H/19 and Room M).

Dup. of Antoninus Pius / *Pietas* lt.?, AD 138-61 (CR Cata 7).

Dup. of Antoninus Pius / *Pax* lt.?, AD 158-61 (CP C/16).

Sest. of Antoninus Pius / *Moneta Aug.* (as *BMC* IV 1253), AD 140-3 (CDF Room Z).

Sest. of Antoninus Pius / Antoninus in chariot rt. (*BMC* IV 1668), AD 148/9 (CDF Room 7?).

As of Antoninus Pius / *Felicitas* rt. (*BMC* IV 1835), AD 145-61 (CDF Room 7).

Sest. of Antoninus Pius / *Pax* lt. (*BMC* IV 1999), AD 156/7 (CR I/18).

Sest. of Antoninus Pius./ *Templum div.Aug.rest.* (*BMC* IV 2045,2065),AD 158/9 (CR I/18)

As of Faustina I / female fig. stg. lt., AD 139-61 (CR H).

Sest. of Diva Faustina I / Temple (as *BMC* IV 1326 (Pius)), AD 141-61 (CR Trench III).

Dup. of Diva Faustina I/ female fig. lt., AD 141-61 (CDF Hoard).

64

Dup. of Diva Faustina I / *Iuno* (*BMC* IV 1396), AD 141-61 (CDF Room B).

As of M. Aurelius Caesar? / female fig. lt.?, AD 140-61 (CR H/15).

As of M. Aurelius Caesar? / female fig. lt. with Victory, AD 140-61 (CR I/20).

Dup. of Faustina II / *Iuno* (as *BMC* IV 2188 (Pius)), AD 146-61 (CR D/180).

2 sest. of Faustina II / female fig. lt., AD 146-61 (CDF Rooms 1 and 7).

Sest. of Faustina II / female fig. std. lt. (as *BMC* IV 1566 (Pius)), AD 146-61 (CDF Hoard).

Denarius of Divus Antoninus / Eagle (*BMC* IV 41 (M. Aur.)), AD 161 (CDF Room B).

Dup. of M. Aurelius / Victory and trophy, AD 161-80 (CR I/20).

As of M. Aurelius / Mars lt. with Victory (*BMC* IV 1083 f.), AD 163/4 (CR I/20).

Sest. of M. Aurelius / Mars rt.? (as *BMC* IV 1072 f.?), AD 163/4 (CR H/17).

As of M. Aurelius / female fig. lt., AD 164 (CR ?).

As of M. Aurelius / Victory lt. (as *BMC* IV 1382), AD 170 (CR Room M).

Sest. of M. Aurelius / Victory rt. (as *BMC* IV 1383 f.), AD 170/1 (CR Trench II).

Sest. of M. Aurelius / *Prov. Deor.*? (as *BMC* IV 1425 f,), AD 171/2 (CR ?).

Sest. of M. Aurelius / *Germania Subacta* (as *BMC* IV 1413), AD 173/4 (CR Trench 1).

As/dup. of M. Aurelius / Roma facing (as *BMC* IV 1487), AD 173/4 (CDF Hoard).

Dup. of M. Aurelius / Trophy and captives (as *BMC* IV 1612 or 1614), AD 176/7 (CR M).

Sest. o£ M. Aurelius / *Felicitati Aug.*: Galley (as *BMC* IV 1615(dup.)) AD 176/7 (CR Hoard).

Sest. of L. Verus / *Fort. Red.* (*BMC* IV 1344*), AD 167/8 (CDF Room B).

Sest. of Faustina II / *Hilaritas* (*BMC* IV 911-3), AD 161-75 (CR I/17).

Sest. of Faustina II / *Iunoni Reginae* (*BMC* IV 921-3), AD 161-75 (CR Room M).

As of Faustina II / *Iuno Regina* (*BMC* IV 985), AD 161-75 (CDF Hoard).

Dup. of Faustina II/ *Saluti Augustae* (*BMC* IV 992), AD 161-75 (CR H/15).

Sest. of Faustina II / *Saluti Augustae* (*BMC* IV 942-8), AD 161-75 (CR H/17).

Sest. of Faustina II / Venus? (as *BMC* IV 955-65?), AD 161-75 (CR G/15).

Sest. of Faustina II / *Venus Felix* (*BMC* IV 957-65), AD 161-75 (CR J/15).

Sest. of Lucilla / *Iunoni Lucinae* (*BMC* IV 1153 (M. Aur.)), AD 169-80 (CR Hoard).

Sest. of Lucilla / *Iunoni Reginae* (*BMC* IV 1153-60), AD 177/8 (CR C/21 A).

Sest. of Commodus / female fig. lt., AD 177-92 (CR Hoard).

Sest. of Commodus / Minerva with Victory rt.?, AD 177-92 (CDF Room 1).

Sest. of Commodus / *Vota Publica* (*BMC* IV 1673 or 1688 (M. Aur.)), AD 177/8 (CR I/15).

As of Commodus / *Vota Publica* (*BMC* IV 1664*), AD 177/8 (CDF Room 5).

Sest. of Commodus / *Iovi Victori* (*BMC* IV 1706 ff,), AD 179/80 (CDF Rooms X-Z).

Sest. of Divus M. Antoninus / Eagle lt.(as *BMC* IV 385-95 (Commodus)),AD 180 (CDF Room ?).

Dup. of Divus M. Antoninus / Eagle lt. (as *BMC* IV 385-95), AD 180 (CR I/17).

Sest. of Commodus / *Prov. Deor.* (as *BMC* IV 494), AD 183 (CDF Hoard).

Dup. of Commodus / Jupiter with Victory lt. (*BMC* IV 498), AD 183 (CR G/10).

As of Commodus / female fig. lt., AD 183-5 (CDF Room 1).

Sest.of Commodus / *Iovi. Exsuper.* (*BMC* IV 586 f.), AD 186 (CR J/20).

Sest.of Commodus / *Securit. Orbis* (*BMC* IV 630), AD 189/90 (CDF Hoard).

2 Asses of Commodus / *Herculi Romano* (*BMC* IV 722-5), AD 191/2 (CR I/12, CDF Room 1).

2 Sest. of Crispina / *Concordia Aug.* (*BMC* IV 406-8), AD 180-3 (CR C/21 and 21 or 22).

6 Roman Imperial Coinage: Septimius Severus to Carinus (104)

Sest. of Septimius Severus / Jupiter lt. with spear, AD 193-211 (CR Hoard).

Sest. of Septimius Severus / female fig. lt. with patera and spear, AD 193-211 (CR Hoard).

Den. of Julia Domna / *Iuno Regina* (as *BMC* V 42 (Sev.)), AD 200-7 (CDF Room D).

As of Julia Domna / *Saeculi Felicitas* (*BMC* V 227 f.(Caracalla)), AD 211-5 (CDF Tr. 9).

As of Caracalla / *Salus* std. lt. (*BMC* V p.345), AD 205 (CR I/15).

Denarius of Caracalla / Galley (*BMC* V 557 (Sev.)), AD 207 (FV).

Denarius of Geta Caesar / *Minerva* (*BMC* 446 (Sev.)), AD 203 (CDF Room Z).

As of Geta Caesar / *Minerva* (*BMC* V 835), AD 203 (CDF Room B).

As of Geta Caeear / *Pietas* (*BMC* V 865), AD 209 (CR I/15 - I/16).

As of Plautilla / *Pietas Augg.* (*BMC* V 804 (Sev.)), AD 203-5 (CR H/16).

Sest. of Julia Soaemias / *Mater Deum* (*BMC* V 373 (Elag.)), AD 218-22 (CR I/18).

As of Severus Alexander / female fig. lt., AD 222-35 (CR I/15-I/16).

Sest. of Severus Alexander / female fig. std. lt., AD 222-35 (CDF Hoard).

Sest. of Severus Alexander / Victory lt., AD 222-35 (CR Hoard).

Denarius (plated?) of Severus Alexander / *Liberalitas Aug.* (as *BMC* VI 3-6), AD 223 or later (J/19).

As of Severus Alexander / *Pax Aug.* (*BMC* VI 100-5), AD 223 (CR J/17).

Sest. of Severus Alexander / Mars rt., (*BMC* VI 250), AD 225 (CR Hoard).

Sest. of Severus Alexander / Victory lt. (as *BMC* VI 274-6), AD 225 (CDF Hoard).

Sest. of Severus Alexander / Victoria Augusti (*BMC* VI 274), AD 225 (CR Hoard).

Sest. of Severus Alexander / Victory lt. (as BMC VI 274-6 or 826), AD 225 or 232 (CDF Hoard)

Sest. of Severus Alexander / *Iustitia Augusti* (*BMC* VI 612-4), AD 230 (CR H/13).

Sest.of Severus Alexander / *Sol* facing (*BMC* VI 625 f.), AD 230-2 (CR H/15).

Sest. of Severus Alexander / Victory lt.(as *BMC* VI 704), AD 231 (CDF Hoard).

Sest. of Severus Alexander / *Iovi Propugnatori* (*BMC* VI 794), AD 231 (CR Hoard).

Sest. of Severus Alexander / *Mars Ultor* (*BMC* VI 840-3), AD 232 (CDF Room B).

Sest of Julia Mamaea / *Venus Genetrix* (*BMC* VI 154 (Alex.), AD 223 (CR Hoard).

Den. of Julia Mamaea / *Fecund. Augustae* (*BMC* VI 113-119) AD 232 (CDF Room Z).

Sest. of Julia Mamaea / *Vesta* (as *BMC* VI 389 or 445) , AD 226/7 (CR Room M).

Sest. of Julia Mamaea / *Felicitas Publica* (*BMC* VI 489-92 or 661-4), AD 228 or 230 (CR H/18).

Sest. of Maximinus / *Victoria Aug.* (*BMC* VI 27 or 108), AD 235/6 (CDF Hoard).

Sest. of Maximinus / *Fides Militum* (as *BMC* V1 2-3 or 63-6), AD 235/6 (CR C/21).

Sest. of Maximinus / *Salus Augusti* (*BMC* VI 100 f.), AD 236 (CR Hoard).

2 Sest. of Maximinus / *Fides Militum* (*BMC* VI 139-41), AD 236 (CDF Hoard: CR H/17).

Sest. of Maximinus / *Pax Augusti* (*BMC* VI 152), AD 236/7 (CR D/21).

Sest. of Maximus Caesar / *Pietas Aug.* (*BMC* VI 119), AD 236 (CR Hoard).

Sest. of Maximus Caesar / *Principi Iuventutis* (*BMC* VI 123f. or 213-7), AD 236/7 (CR Hoard).

Sest. of Gordian III / female fig. lt., AD 238-44 (CR H/17).

Sest. of Gordian III / female fig. lt., AD 238-44 (CDF Hoard).

As of Gordian III / Mars rt.?, AD 238-44 (CR I/12).

Denarius of Gordian III / uncertain reverse, AD 238-44 (CR I/19).

Sest. of Gordian III / *Pax Augusti* (*RIC* IV 256a), AD 238/9 (CR Hoard).

Sest. of Gordian III / *Iovi Conservatori* (*RIC* IV 255a), AD 238/9 (CR Hoard).

Sest. of Gordian III / *Concordia Aug.* (*RIC* IV 287), AD 240 (CR J/17).

Sest. of Gordian III/ Gordian sacrificing lt.? (as *RIC* IV 271), AD 240? (CR H/17).

As of Gordian III / Gordian sacrificing lt.? (as *RIC* IV 292b), AD 240? (CR H/17).

Sest. of Gordian III / Gordian sacrificing lt. (as *RIC* IV 280), AD 240 (CR Hoard).

Sest. of Gordian III / Gordian sacrificing lt. (*RIC* IV 292a), AD 240 (CDF Hoard).

4 sest. of Gordian III / Apollo throned lt. (as *RIC* IV 301-4), AD 241-3 (CR C/21A, CR Trench III, CR Hoard (2)).

2 sest. of Gordian III / *Mars Propugnat.* (*RIC* IV 332a), AD 243 (CR I/19).

Antoninianus of Gordian III / *Securit. Perp.* (as *RIC* IV 151-3), AD 243/4 (CR C/16).

Sest. of Philip I / *Aequitas Augg.* (*RIC* IV 166), AD 244-9 (CDF Hoard).

Antoninianus of Philip I / Victory ? (as *RIC* IV 49-51?), AD 244-9 (CR Cata 8).

Sest. of Philip I / Philip std. lt. with globe (*RIC* IV 148), AD 245 (CR H/15).

2 antoniniani of Philip I / *Felicitas* lt. (*RIC* IV 4), AD 247 (CR I/18 and I/19).

2 sest. of Philip I / *Saeculares Augg.* (*RIC* IV 160a), AD 248 (CR H/19 and J/21).

Sest. of Philip I / *Liberalitas Augg.* (as *RIC* IV 182), AD 248/9 (CR Hoard).

Sest. of Otacilia Severa / *Concordia Augg.* (*RIC* IV 203a-b), AD 244-9 (CR Hoard).

Sest. of Otacilia Severa / *Pietas Augg.* (*RIC* IV 198), AD 248 (CR H/15).

Sest. of Philip II Caesar / *Principi Iuvent.* (*RIC* IV 255a), AD 244-6 (CDF Trench 12).

2 sest. of Philip II Caesar / *Principi Iuventutis* (*RIC* IV 257a), AD 244-6 (CDF Hoard, CR Hoard).

Antoninianus of Philip II Augustus / *Saeculares Augg.* (*RIC* IV 224), AD 248 (CR Room?).

Sest. of Trajan Decius / *Dacia* (*RIC* IV 112a-b), AD 249-51 (CR Hoard).

Dup.? of Trajan Decius / *Liberalitas Aug.* (*RIC* IV 120c), AD 249-51 (CDF Hoard).

Sest. of Trajan Decius / *Victoria Aug.* (*RIC* IV 108a or c), AD 249-51 (CR Hoard).

Sest. of Herennia Etruscilla / *Pudicitia Aug.* (*RIC* IV 136b(Dec.)), AD 249-51 (CR I/18).

Sest. of Trebonianus Gallus / female fig. lt., AD 251-3 (CR Hoard).

3 sest. of Trebonianus Gallus / *Liberalitas Augg.* (*RIC* IV 113), AD 251-3 (CR Hoard, CDF Rooms B and I).

Sest. of Trebonianus Gallus / *Votis Decennalibus* (*RIC* IV 127), AD 251 (CR H).

Sest. of Trebonianus Gallus / *Pietas Augg.* (*RIC* IV 116a), AD 251 (CR I/17).

As of Trebonianus Gallus / *Virtus Augg.* (*RIC* IV 126a), AD 252 (CR H/18).

Sest. of Trebonianus Gallus / *Iunoni Martiali* (*RIC* IV 110a), AD 252 (CR C/21).

Sest. of Trebonianus Gallus / *Aeternitas Augg.* (*RIC* IV 102), AD 253 (CDF Hoard).

Sest. of Valerian / *Concordiae Augg.* (*RIC* V 154), AD 253/4 (CR Hoard).

Antoninianus of Gallienus / *Virtus Augg.* (*RIC* V 455(Val.):eastern mint), AD 253/4 (CDF Hoard).

Sest. of Salonina / *Iuno Regina* (*RIC* V 46 (Val.)), AD 253/4 (CR G).

Antoninianus of Gallienus / *Oriens Aug.* (*RIC* V 249), AD 265/6 (CR I/11-J/11).

Antoninianus of Gallienus / *Apollini cons. Aug.* (*RIC* V 167), AD 267/8 (CR Temple 2).

Antoninianus of Gallienus / *Dianae cons.Aug.* (*RIC* V 180), AD 267/8 (CR H/19).

Antoninianus of Salonina / ---- *cons. Aug.* (*RIC* V 4 or 14-6), AD 267/8 (CR G/10).

Antoninianus of Salonina / *Iunoni cons. Aug.* (*RIC* V 16), AD 267/8 (CR F/11).

Antoninianus of Claudius II / uncertain, AD 268-70 (CR I/100).

Antoninianus of Claudius II / *Fides Exerci.* (*RIC* V 34-6), AD 268? (CR Trench II).

Antoninianus of Claudius II / *Pax Augusti* (*RIC* V 82), AD 268? (CR H/13).

Antoninianus of Claudius II / *Virtus Augusti* (*RIC* V 113), AD 268-70 (CR I/18).

Antoninianus of Claudius II / *Providen. Aug.* (*RIC* V 187 (Sis.)), AD 269/70? (CR G/15).

Antoninianus of Claudius II / *Virtuti Aug.* (*RIC* V 255 (Cyz.)), AD 268-70 (CR G/15).

Denarius of Aurelian / *Victoria Aug.* (*RIC* V 39 var.), AD 274/5 (CR I/20).

3 barbarous copies of *Divo Claudio* antoninianus (Altar), c. AD 274-80 (CDF Well 2, CR G/11, and H/15).

Reform coin of Tacitus / *Salus Publica* (*RIC* V 159b(Tic.)), AD 275/6 (CR G/15).

Reform coin of Probus / *Fides Militum* (*RIC* V 169), AD 276-82 (CR Trench I).

Reform coin of Probus / *Salus Aug.* (*RIC* V 744 (Rome)), AD 276-82 (CR H).

Reform coin of Probus / *Soli Invicto* (*RIC* V 208), AD 276-82 (CV '73).

7. Roman Imperial Coinage: Diocletian to Constantius II (12)

Radiate billon of Maximian / *Vot. XX* enclosed in wreath (as *RIC* VI 74 ff.), AD 297/8 (CR H).

Follis of Maxentius / *Conservatores urbis suae?* (as *RIC* VI 162), AD 307 (CR C/16).

4 reduced folles of Constantine I / *Soli Invicto comiti* (as *RIC* VI 120 ff.), AD 309-18 (CR Area 1-2, G/10, H/19, I/15-J/15).

Follis of Constantine I / *Vota XXX* in wreath (as *RIC* VII 322), AD 329/30 (CR Trench II).

Reduced follis of Constantine I / *Gloria exercitus* (one standard: as *RIC* VII 381), AD 336/7 (CR Trench II).

Reduced follis of Constantius II / *Victoriae DD Augg. q. nn.* (as *LRBC* 1.705), AD 341-8 (CR I/10).

3 AE 3 of Constantius II / *Fel. temp. reparatio* (Fallen Horseman: as *LRBC* 2.682 ff. (CR D/19, CDF '76, CB).

8. Roman Imperial Coinage: House of Valentinian and Theodosius I (4)

AE 3 of Valens / *Gloria Romanorum* (as *LRBC* 2.703), AD 364-78 (CR E/10).

AE 3 of Valentinian II / *Gloria Romanorum* ? (as *LRBC* 2.729?), AD 375-8 or 383-7 (CR E/11).

AE 4 of Valentinian II / *Vot. X mult. XX* (as *LRBC* 2.1076 or 1097), AD 378-83 or 383-7 (CR Trench I).

AE 4 of Theodosius I / *Victoria Auggg.* (as *LRBC* 2.780), AD 383-7 (CR Trench II).

9. Mediaeval Coinage (2)

2 mediaeval croats: King's head (facing: lt.) / cross (CR C/17 and Trench VIII).

BIBLIOGRAPHY

ACUÑA FERNANDEZ, P., 1975: *Esculturas militares romanas de España y Portugal, I - Las esculturas thoracatas*, Biblioteca de la Escuela Española de Historia y Arqueología en Roma, C.S.I.C., Madrid.

ADAM, J. P. 1994: *Roman building : materials and techniques*. Bloomington : Indiana University Press,.

ADAM, J. P. 1984: *La construction romaine. Materiaux et techniques*. Grands Manuels Picard, Paris (Edi. español 1996, León).

ALMAGRO, M.; AMOROS, L. R., 1953-54: "Excavaciones en la necrópolis romana de Ca'n Fanals de *Pollentia* (Alcudia, Mallorca)." *Ampurias,* XV-XVI, pp. 237-277, Barcelona.

ALMAGRO, M.; AMOROS, L., 1955: "El teatro romano de *Pollentia* (Mallorca)." *III Congreso Arqueológico Nacional*, Galicia 1953, pp. 187-195, Zaragoza.

AMORÓS, L. R., 1944-46: "Excavaciones en Pollentia en 1944," *BSAL* 29, pp. 144-146.

AMORÓS, L.R., 1947-1952: "Excavaciones en Pollentia. Antecedentes. Campaña de excavaciones arqueológicas de 1948," *BSAL* 30, pp. 434-442.

AMOROS, L.; ALMAGRO, M.; ARRIBAS, A., 1954a: *Excavación del teatro romano de Pollentia 1953*. The Willian L. Bryant Foundation, Palma.

AMOROS, L.; ALMAGRO, M.; ARRIBAS, A., 1954b: "El teatro romano de Pollentia," *AEA* 27, pp. 281-299.

ARCE, J., 1981: "El significado religioso del estandarte romano de *Pollentia*." *La religión romana en España*, pp. 77-84, Madrid.

ARCE, J., 1984: "A Roman Bronze Standard from *Pollentia* (Mallorca) and the *Collegia Iuvenum*." A.A.V.V., *Toreutik und figürliche Bronzen römischen Zeit*, pp. 33-40. Staatliche Museen. Antikenmuseum, Berlin.

ARRIBAS, A., TARRADELL, M. and WOODS, D., 1973: *Pollentia I. Excavaciones en Sa Portella. Alcúdia (Mallorca)*. Excavaciones Arqueológicas en España, nº 75, Madrid.

ARRIBAS, A., TARRADELL, M. and WOODS, D., 1978a: *Pollentia II. Excavaciones en Sa Portella. Alcúdia (Mallorca)*. Excavaciones Arqueológicas en España, nº 98, Madrid.

ARRIBAS, A., 1978b: "La Arqueología de *Pollentia*." TARRADELL, ARRIBAS y ROSSELLÓ-BORDOY, *Historia de Alcudia*, tomo I, pp. 111-291, Ayuntamiento de Alcudia, Mallorca.

ARRIBAS, A., 1983a: *La romanització de les Illes Balears*. Llicó inaugural del curs 1983-84, Palma.

ARRIBAS, A., 1983b: "*Pollentia*: Problemas de topografía y conservación de la ciudad." *Symposium de arqueología. Pollentia y la romanización de las Baleares*, Alcudia, 1977, pp. 35-46, Mallorca.

ARRIBAS, A. (Ed.), 1983c: *Pollentia. Estudio de los materiales I*. The William L. Bryant Foundation 3, Palma.

ARRIBAS, A. and LLABRES, J., 1983d: "Una necrópolis romana en el *Ager Pollentino. Pollentia."*

Estudio de los materiales, I. Sa *Portella, excavaciones 1957-1963*, pp. 303-365, Palma.

ARRIBAS, A. and TARRADELL, M., 1987: "El foro de *Pollentia*. Noticia de las primeras investigaciones." *Los foros romanos de las Provincias Occidentales*, pp.121-136, Madrid.

ARRIBAS, A., 1993: "Una Reja de Ventana Romana Procedente de *Pollentia* (Mallorca)," *Homenatge a Miquel Tarradell*, pp. 779-792. Barcelona.

ARRIBAS, A. and DOENGES, N. A., 1995: "Piezas singulares de una estancia del área del foro de *Pollentia*." *1º Congreso de Arqueología Peninsular*, Actas V, Trabalhos de Antropologia e Etnologia, vol. 35 (1), pp. 397-420, Porto.

BERGMANN, M., 1990: *Römische Reiterstatue*. Beiträge zur Erschließung hellenistischer und kaiserzeitlicher Skulptur und Architektur II. Editorial Ph. von Zabern, Mainz/Rhein.

BINIMELIS, J.B., 1927: *Nueva Historia de la Isla de Mallorca I*. Palma.

BROWN, F., 1980: *Cosa: The Making of a Roman Town,* Ann Arbor.

CARDELL, J. and ORFILA, M., 1991-2: "Posible catastro romano en la isla de Mallorca." *Cuadernos de Prehistoria y Arqueología,* 16-17, pp. 415-423, Universidad de Granada, Granada.

CERDA I JUAN, D., 1999: *El vi en l'ager pollentinus i en el seu entorn*. Col.lecció La Deixa, 3. Monografies de Patrimoni Històric, Palma.

COLL, J., MAZAIRA, L. and RIUTORT, S., 1984: "Evolución del hábitat durante la prehistoria y la antigüedad en el término municipal de Alcudia." *Arqueología Espacial*, 2, pp. 111-129, Teruel.

COMFORT, H., 1961: "Roman Ceramics in Spain: an exploratory visit," *AEA* 34, pp. 3-17.

CURCHIN, L. A., 1991: *Roman Spain: Conquest and Assimilation*. London.

DOENGES, N. A., 2005: *The William L. Bryant Foundation: a Brief History,* Hanover, NH.

EQUIP D'EXCAVACIONS DE *POLLENTIA*, 1993: "Un conjunt de materials d'època tardo-republicana de la ciutat romana de *Pollentia* (Alcudia, Mallorca)." *Pyrenae*, 24, pp. 227-267, Barcelona.

EQUIP D'EXCAVACIONS DE *POLLENTIA*, 1994a: "Resultats dels treballs d'excavació a l'àrea central de la ciutat romana de *Pollentia* (Alcudia, Mallorca): avanç preliminar." *Pyrenae*, 25, pp. 215-224, Barcelona.

EQUIP D'EXCAVACIONS DE *POLLENTIA*, 1994b: "Avanç dels resultats dels treballs d'excavació a l'àrea central de la ciutat romana de Pol.lentia." *XIV Congreso Internacional de Arqueología Clásica. La ciudad en el mundo romano*, vol. 2, pp. 140-142, Tarragona.

FERNANDEZ-MIRANDA, M., 1983: "Las cerámicas talayóticas procedentes de la calle Porticada." A. Arribas (Ed.) *Pollentia. Estudio de los materiales I.*

The William L. Bryant Foundation 3, pp. 11-45. Palma.

GARCÍA y BELLIDO, A., 1949: *Esculturas romanas de España y Portugal.* C.S.I.C., Madrid.

GARCÍA y BELLIDO, A., 1951: "Esculturas romanas de Pollentia (La Alcudia, Mallorca)" *AEA* 24, pp.53-65.

GARCÍA y BELLIDO, A., 1959: "Las colonias romanas de Hispania." *Anuario de Historia del Derecho Español,* XXIX, Madrid.

GARCÍA RIAZA, E., 1999a: "La *civitas Bocchoritana:* una cuestión abierta," *Revista d'Arqueologia de Ponent* n. 9, pp. 59-71. Universitat de Lleida.

GARCÍA RIAZA, E., 1999b: "Ciudades federadas de Baleares en la antigüedad," *Mayurqa* 25, pp. 169-176. Palma de Mallorca.

GARCIA RIAZA, E. and SÁNCHEZ, LEÓN, M.L., 2000: *Roma y la municipalización de las Baleares,* Col.lecció 2000 y UIB, 2, Universitat de les Illes Balears, Palma.

GUMÀ, M. M.; RIERA, M. M.; TORRES, X., 1997: "Contextos ceràmics dels segles IV-X a l'illa de Mallorca. Contextos ceràmics d'època romano tardana i de l'Alta Edat Mitjana (segles IV-X)," *ArqueoMediterrània,* 2, pp. 249-269, Universitat de Barcelona. Barcelona.

GURT, J. M. and MAROT, T., 1994: "Estudi dels models de circulació monetària a les Balears: *Pollentia* (Alcudia, Mallorca). III Reunió d'Arqueología Cristiana e Hispànica (Menorca 1988)," *Mongrafies de la secció Historico-Arqueològica,* II, pp. 223-234, Barcelona.

KEAY, S.J., 1988: *Roman Spain.* Berkeley.

KNAPP, R. C., 1977: *Aspects of the Roman experience in Iberia, 206-100 B.C.* Valladolid.

LLABRÉS BERNAL, J. and R. ISASI RANSOME, 1939: "Excavaciones en los terrenos donde estuvo enclavada la ciudad romana de Pollentia (Baleares, Isla de Mallorca, Término municipal de Alcudia)" *Memoria de los trabajos practicados en 1930 1931,* Memoria 131, Madrid.

MANCILLA, M.I., 2001: La Habitació Z y el Pórtico de la Calle Oeste de la Ínsula de *Tabernae* al Oeste del Foro de la ciudad romana de *Pollentia* (Alcudia, Mallorca). La vajilla de Barniz Negro. Memoria de Licenciatura. Universidad de Granada. Dactilografiada.

MAR, R. and ROCA, M., 1998: "Pollentia y Tárraco. Dos etapas en la formación de los foros de la Hispania Romana." *Ampurias,* 51, Diputación de Barcelona, pp. 105-124, Barcelona.

MAROT, M.T., 1990: "Monedes vàndales i bizantines a Pollentia." *Gaceta Numismatica,* 99, IV-90, pp. 29-33, Barcelona.

MAROT, T., 1997: "Aproximación a la circulación monetaria en la Península Ibérica y las islas Baleares durante los siglos V y VI: la incidencia de las emisiones vándalas y bizantinas." *Revue Numismatique,* vol 152, pp. 157-190, Paris.

MAROT, T., 2000: "Monedes procedents de *Pollentia* (Alcúdia, Mallorca): campanyes 1996-1999)," ORFILA, Ed., *El fòrum de* Pollentia. *Memòria de les campanyes..,* pp. 175-182. Ajuntament d'Alcúdia. Alcudia.

MAS FORNERS, A., 1999: "El segle XIII," en *Història d'Alcudia. De l'època islàmica a la germania* de A. Mas, G. Rosselló y R. Rosselló, Ajuntament d'Alcúdia, Alcúdia, pp. 45-88.

MASSNER, A. K., 1982: *Bildnisangleichung. Untersuchungen zur Entstehungs- und Wirkungsgeschichte der Augustusporträts (43 v. Ch.-68 n. Chr).* Das Römische Herrscherbild, IV, DAI, Berlin.

MATTINGLY, H., 1983: "Roman Pollentia: coinage and history." ARRIBAS, Ed., *Pollentia. Estudio de los materiales I.* The William L. Bryant Foundation 3, pp. 243-301. Palma.

MAYER, M. and RODÁ, I., 1983: "Consideraciones sobre el topónimo Pollentia y el asentamiento romano en la bahía de Pollensa." *Symposium de Arqueología. Pollentia y la Romanización de las Baleares,* pp. 23-34, Ayuntamiento de Alcudia, Mallorca.

MORANTA, L., 1997: *El teatro romano de Palma. Una hipótesis y sus primeras comprobaciones.* Col.legi Oficial d'Arquitectes de Balears, Palma de Mallorca.

MORANTA, L.; ORFILA. M., 2002: "El traçat regulador del Fòrum de Pol.lèntia." *II Jornades d'Estudis Locals d'Alcúdia,* pp. 129-146. Ajuntament d'Alcúdia. Mallorca.

MORGAN, M. G., 1969: "The Roman Conquest of the Balearic Isles." *Calif. Studies in Classical Antiquity* 2, pp. 217-231.

ORFILA, M. (ed.), 2000: *El fòrum de Pollentia. Memòria de les campanyes d'excavacions realitzades entre els anys 1996 i 1999,* Ajuntament d'Alcúdia, Àrea de Patrimoni.

ORFILA, M. and ARRIBAS, A., 1997: "La ciudad romana de Pollentia (Alcudia, Mallorca) en la actualidad." *Congreso ciudades históricas vivas. Ciudades del pasado: pervivencia y desarrollo,* Mérida 1997, pp. 63-67, Museo Nacional de Arte Romano, Mérida.

ORFILA, M., ARRIBAS, A. and CAU, M. A., 1999: "El foro romano de *Pollentia.*" *Archivo Español de Arqueología,* LXXII, pp. 99-118, Consejo Superior de Investigaciones Científicas, Madrid.

ORFILA, M., ARRIBAS, A. and DOENGES, N. A., 1999: "El forum de la ciutat romana de *Pollentia,* estat actual de les excavacions." *I Jornades d'Estudis Locals,* noviembre de 1998, pp. 85-100, Alcudia, Mallorca.

ORFILA, M. and MORANTA, L., 2001: "Estudio del trazado regulador del Foro de *Pollentia* (Alcúdia, Mallorca)," *Archivo Español de Arqueología,* 74, pp. 209-232, CSIC, Madrid.

ORFILA, M. and RIERA, M., 2002: "Alguns vestigis d'època islàmica al fòrum de Pollentia," *Homenatje a Guillem Rosselló Bordoy,* Govern de les Illes Balears. Conselleria d'Educació i Cultura. Palma, pp. 705-724.

ORFILA, M.; RIERA, M.; CAU, M. A.; ARRIBAS, A., 2000: "Aproximación a la topografía urbana tardía de Pollentia (Mallorca): Construcciones defensivas." *IV Reunió d'Arqueologia Cristiana Hispánica*, (Cartagena 1998), pp. 229-235. Institut d'Estudis Catalans, Barcelona.

PALANQUES, M. L., 1992: *Las lucernas de Pollentia*. The William Bryant Foundation 4, Palma.

PARMENT, T.W., 1995: *The Capitolium of Pollentia*, Dissertation presented to the Department of Classics, Dartmouth College, Hanover, N.H.

PREVOSTI, M. and RAFEL, N., 1983: "Introducción al estudio de las esculturas romanas de *Pollentia*," *Symposium de arqueología. Pollentia y la romanización de las Baleares*, pp. 167-186. Alcudia 1977, Ayuntamiento de Alcudia, Mallorca.

PRIETO, A., 1987-88: "Un punto oscuro en la invasión romana de las Baleares: la piratería." *Habis*, 18-19, pp. 271-275, Universidad de Sevilla, Sevilla.

RICHARDSON, J. S., 1986: *Hispaniae, Spain and the development of Roman imperialism, 218-82 BC*. Cambridge [Cambridgeshire]. New York.

RIERA, M.; CAU, M. A. and ORFILA, M., 1999: "Els ultims segles de *Pollentia*." *Bolletí de la Societat Arqueològica Lul.liana*, 55, pp. 335-346. Palma de Mallorca.

ROCA, M. and SUBÍAS, E., 1996/97: "La Casa dels Dos Tresors de Pollentia: Una reflexió." *Annals de l'Institut d'Estudis Gironins*, XXXVII, pp. 825-837, Gerona.

RODÁ, I., 1990: "Los bronces romanos de la Hispania Citerior. A.A.V.V.," *Los bronces romanos en España*, pp. 71-90, Ministerio de Cultura, Madrid.

ROSSELLÓ BORDOY, G., 1982: "El portaviandas medieval de Pollentia (Alcudia/Mallorca)." *Boletín de la Sociedad Arqueológica Luliana*, 39, pp. 23-28, Palma.

SANCHEZ LEÓN, Mª L. y GARCÍA RIAZA, E., 2002: "Un nuevo duunviro de *Pollentia* (Alcudia, Mallorca)," *Homenatje a Guillem Rosselló Bordoy*, pp. 903-910. Govern de les Illes Balears. Conselleria d'Educació i Cultura. Palma.

SANMARTÍ, J., PRINCIPAL, J., TRÍAS. GL. and ORFILA, M., 1996: *Les ceràmiques de vernís negre de Pollentia*. The William L. Bryant Foundation 5, Barcelona.

SUBÍAS, E., 1994: "Anàlisi metrològica del capitoli. Equip d'excavacions de *Pollentia*, 1994a: Resultats dels treballs d'excavació a l'àrea central de la ciutat romana de *Pollentia* (Alcúdia, Mallorca): avanç preliminar." *Pyrenae* 25, pp. 220-224, Universidad de Barcelona, Barcelona.

TARRADELL, M., 1978a: "Primeres noticies de la crisi del segle III d. C. a Mallorca." *Memoria del Institut d'Arqueología i Prehistoria*, pp. 27-32, Barcelona.

TARRADELL, M., 1978b: "*Pollentia*. Esquema de una aproximación histórica." TARRADELL, ARRIBAS y ROSSELLÓ-BORDOY, *Historia de Alcudia*, tomo I, pp. 295-357, Ayuntamiento de Alcudia, Mallorca.

TARRADELL, M., 1978c: *Les ciutats romanes del Paisos Catalans*. Reial Acadèmia de Bones Lletres de Barcelona, Barcelona.

TARRADELL, M., ARRIBAS, A., ROSSELLÓ-BORDOY, G., 1978: *Historia de Alcudia*, tomo I, Ayuntamiento de Alcudia, Mallorca.

ULRICH, R., 1996: "*Contignatio*, Vitruvius, and the Campanian Builder," *AJA* 100, pp. 137-151.

VENTAYOL SUAU, P., 1927: *Historia de Alcudia*, Palma.

VENY, C., 1965: *Corpus de las inscripciones baleáricas hasta la dominación árabe*. Madrid.

VERMEULE, C. C. 1959/60: "Hellenistic and Roman Cuirassed Statues." *Berytus*, col. XIII, pp. 3-82. The Museum of Archeology of The American University of Beirut, Copenhagen.

WILSON, A. J. N., 1966: *Emigration from Italy in the Republican age of Rome*. Manchester, New York.

ZANKER, P., 1973: *Studien zu den Augustus-Portäts. I. Der Actium Typus*. Abhandlungen ser Akademie der Wissenschaften in Götingen 85, Götingen.

ZUCCA, R., 1998: *Insulae Baleares. Le isole Baleari sotto dominio romano*. Cariocci Editore, Roma.

www.ingramcontent.com/pod-product-compliance
Lightning Source LLC
Chambersburg PA
CBHW061304270326
41932CB00029B/3470